WE HAVE
THIS HERITAGE

□□□

CLYDE L. MANSCHRECK

GRADED PRESS
NASHVILLE, TENNESSEE

WE HAVE THIS HERITAGE

A study book

Copyright © 1968 by Graded Press

A publication of The Methodist Church prepared by the General Board of Education through the Editorial Division and published by Graded Press, the curriculum publishing department of The Methodist Publishing House, 201 Eighth Ave. So., Nashville, Tennessee 37203. Printed in the United States of America.

Unless otherwise noted Scripture quotations are from the Revised Standard Version of the Bible copyright 1946 and 1952 by the Division of Christian Education of the National Council of Churches, and used by permission.

☐ Henry M. Bullock is editor of church school publications, Editorial Division, Methodist Board of Education. ☐ Horace R. Weaver is editor of adult publications. ☐ Harold L. Fair is editor of Foundation Studies in Christian Faith, the series of which *We Have This Heritage* is the third part.

TO MY STUDENTS
WITH WHOM I HAVE ENJOYED
REDISCOVERING OUR HERITAGE

CONTENTS

EDITOR'S INTRODUCTION

The book you are now reading is the third study book in a new curriculum series, Foundation Studies in Christian Faith. A new part (or unit) will be issued three months from the publication of this part and for each succeeding three months until eight parts have been published. The other seven parts are described on the inside front cover of this book. The series—Foundation Studies in Christian Faith —therefore is an eight-part study that may extend for two years if a new part is begun every three months.

The components. There are three "components" to each part of the study:

—the study book (which you are now reading)
—the book of selected readings
—the resource packet for leaders of adult groups

These three components make up one part. Each three months a new study book, a new book of selected readings, and a new resource packet for leaders of adult groups will be issued. The three components in each quarterly part have the same title. For example, the book of selected readings and

7

the resource packet to accompany this book are also entitled *We Have This Heritage.*

The study book. As you turn through this study book, you will notice several distinguishing features. At the beginning of each chapter, reference is made to several biblical passages. Read these passages in your Bible before you read the chapter. We recommend the *Oxford Annotated Bible,* Revised Standard Version (Oxford University Press) or the *Harper Study Bible,* Revised Standard Version (Zondervan Publishing House) for home use by every member of the class. (Available from Cokesbury.) Bible study is an important part of this unit. Members of the group might be asked to bring their own Bibles or the group might purchase inexpensive copies and have them available at the place of meeting for each session.

When you come to an asterisk (*), turn to the end of the chapter. There you will find the notes which give the sources of the quotations.

Leadership procedures. You will notice as you look through this book that certain paragraphs have a small black square (■) at the beginning. These paragraphs suggest a wide variety of ways of reacting to the ideas raised in the material. It is not expected that a group will use every suggestion or procedure. The procedures are placed in the study book to encourage each member of the group to assume responsibility for discussion and to stimulate thinking as you read the book. There is no separate book for leaders only. Leaders and other members of the group should each have personal copies of both the study book and the book of selected readings. Only the designated leader or "teaching team," however, will receive the resource packet described below for use with the group. The packet contains a leaders' guide.

At the center of this book and the book of selected readings you will find a section of pictures. The pictures in this book comprise a historical survey of the story of the church. Those in the book of selected readings illustrate some of the new ways in which the mission of the church is being carried forward today.

Included in the resource packet for leaders of adult groups are two recordings—one to be used with the pictures in this book and the other to accompany the pictures in the book of selected readings.

These recordings are to be used with the pictures in very much the same way as a script is used with the frames of a filmstrip. That is, you, the reader, will turn through the pictures as the recording tells the story.

The pictures in this book and the accompanying narration are closely related, dependent on each other. The second recording and the pictures in the book of selected readings are more loosely related. In fact, the second recording can be used and understood apart from the pictures. ·

The leaders' guide in the resource packet for leaders of adult groups contains imaginative and thorough suggestions and directions for deriving the greatest benefit from this unique tool.

On the first page of each chapter, reference is made to an "assignment chart." This chart may be on a sheet of posterboard or newsprint or a chalkboard. It might suggest, for instance, a question to think about before the session begins. At the first session, the leader might explain to the group that he will have the chart prepared and posted before each session so that preparation for the discussion can begin as soon as each member arrives.

At the end of each chapter the suggestion is made that the leader be ready to make assignments for the next session and that members of the group be prepared to accept such assignments. Advance assignments increase the ability of the group to make the most efficient use possible of the discussion period. These assignments also suggest a variety of ways to get before the group information not included in the text itself, such as the opinions of persons outside the group or relevant facts regarding your local community or church. To make the most profitable use of assignments, the leader or leadership team should go through the entire book in their planning in order to work out assignments which would be most valuable for the group.

Leaders are not expected to use *every* procedure in this book. A large number of procedures are suggested in order that the leader and the group may *choose* those most interesting and relevant to them. A word of caution: every procedure in the book assumes that the members of the group are familiar with the text. If members have not read the text, many procedures will lose most of their significance and meaning. Encourage every member of the group to read the assigned portion of this book (and the relevant sections of the book of selected readings if the group is using that book) *in advance* of the session.

The leader or leadership team should also note as they prepare before the beginning of the study which supplies will be needed. Someone should be designated to have the supplies at the place of meeting at the proper time. These supplies might include a record player for using the plastic records in the resource packet; a chalkboard, chalk, and an eraser; or a newsprint pad and dark crayon or other type of marker; Bibles; and other materials at the discretion of the leader. (A newsprint pad, an inexpensive pad of rough paper available from most stationery stores, has the advantage of being portable.)

The book of selected readings. Each person in the group should have a copy of the book of selected readings with the same title as this study book, *We Have This Heritage.* In the book of selected readings, you will find a wide variety of selections from a number of other printed resources relevant to the study of our heritage in the church. While it is not absolutely essential for every person to have a copy of the book of selected readings, the study will be significantly enriched if this study book and the book of selected readings are read and used together. They are companion volumes. Many procedures involve use of selected readings. In this study book you will frequently see the abbreviation *S/R* followed by a number. When you come to a place in the text where this abbreviation appears, turn to the book of selected readings and find the reading whose number corresponds to the one following the abbreviation *S/R*. The book of selected readings has no page numbers—rather, the selections are numbered.

The resource packet. In addition to a new study book and a new book of selected readings each three months, a resource packet for leaders will be issued, having the same title as the study book and the book of selected readings. Each group will need one packet with the same title as this study book, *We Have This Heritage.*

The editorial team that developed this unit was Lon A. Speer (resource packet), Judith Weidman (book of selected readings), Harold D. Minor and Nellie Moser (leadership procedures), Mary Alice Asbury (manuscript editor), and Horace R. Weaver. Dan Brawner and Richard Elliott were responsible for the design and layout. Mrs. Jeanne Arnold faithfully typed and retyped the manuscript. The standard and style for this unit were set by the Methodist Board of Education.

HAROLD L. FAIR

PHOTO CREDITS
1. *Christ Crucified Between Two Thieves,* by Peter Paul Rubens; 3. "An Early Christian Martyrdom," from *The Story of the Church* by Walter Russell Bowie. Copyright 1955 by Pierce and Washabaugh (Abingdon Press); 4. Ewing Galloway; 5. *Saint Jerome in His Cell,* by Albrecht Durer; 6. *Saint Augustine,* by Giuseppe Ribera; 7. Screen Traveler from Gendreau; 8. Black Star; 12. "Hawking Indulgences," from *Here I Stand* by Roland H. Bainton. Copyright 1950 by Pierce and Smith (Abingdon Press); 13. Ewing Galloway; 14. Religious News Service Photo; 15. Zintgraff; 16. Reproduced from the collections of the Library of Congress; 17. "Wesley Preaching to a Mob," courtesy of *Together Magazine.* Copyright 1963 by The Methodist Publishing House; 18. Dan Brawner; 19. Reproduced from the collections of the Library of Congress; 20. Methodist Missions; 21. Reproduced from the collections of the Library of Congress; 22. Reproduced from the collections of the Library of Congress; 23. Reproduced from the collections of the Library of Congress; 24. Methodist Information.

AUTHOR'S PREFACE

". . . If I could only remember who I am!" cries the victim of amnesia. He has lost his memory; therefore, he does not know his life story. That is, he does not know who he is. Since his past is lost, he does not know how to begin anew.

When a person thinks about problems before him, he recalls from his memory past experiences relevant to his present situation. If he has no memory, he is like a child— for one characteristic of childhood is that there are few experiences on which to draw. The child has not yet learned fully to use his past for meeting his present crises. As he matures, he learns that the past is valuable to him in solving new problems.

When we face a crucial situation, we "stop to think." An important historian of our time has said that one cannot think unless he is aware of past experiences. ". . . Knowing yourself means knowing what you can do; and since nobody knows what he can do until he tries, the only clue about what man can do is what man has done." *

If we do know the past, we will better understand not only the present moment but also the possibilities open to us in the future. If we do not know the past—and the church is *our* past as Christians—we are like that victim of amnesia. Not knowing where we have come from, we do not know how to go on from here.

This book does not, however, focus on the past. Its view is on the church today—what it is and what it shall become. The subtitle of this volume is "The Church as Witness to the Good News." Sometimes that witness has been glorious; at other times, it has been shameful. Is the church today witnessing to the good news in a way that brings glory to God? If we can discover the causes for shame in the past as well as how the church has exalted God, we shall better understand how the church in our time can be a glorious witness to the good news.

This book is about an inheritance. That heritage is the church. The church has been given to us by God. To appreciate this gift, we must know better what it is—and one way of learning what it is, is to study its life story.

This study, it is hoped, will help you grow in your understanding of the church as a community of people called by and responding to God and thereby help you become a more faithful witness to the good news in our time.

Clyde L. Manschreck

Chicago Theological Seminary
Chicago, Illinois

NOTE

Page 12: R. G. Collingwood, *The Idea of History* (Oxford University Press, 1946), page 10 (Galaxy edition). Used by permission.

Read these selections in your Bible:
Ecclesiastes 1:1–3:9
The futility of life.

Luke 23:32–24:53
The crucifixion and the empty tomb.

1 Corinthians 15:1-58
Destruction of the last enemy.

I John 4:7-21
"If God so loved us."

Acts 2:1-47
The Day of Pentecost.

1

□□

THE COMMUNITY OF THE RESURRECTION

"Mother died today. Or maybe, yesterday; I can't be sure." * So begins the novel *The Stranger* by Albert Camus. The story is of Meursault, a man caught in life's grip, a man who finally faces death for a senseless murder. When the chaplain visits his prison cell, they quarrel. Meursault suddenly realizes that the truth behind everything is indifference. The universe is indifferent. "Nothing, nothing had the least importance, and I knew quite well why." * All alike die, "the same thing for Salamano's wife and for Salamano's dog." * The discovery makes Meursault feel free. In life or in death nothing makes any difference whatsoever.

HOW IT BEGAN

Within a few blocks or miles of where you live is a church. Or perhaps many churches. Whatever the name of the church

---

■ *In the room where your group is meeting, display a large poster on which are written assignments for specific preparation to be made by the members of the group before the session begins.*

14

on the sign in the churchyard, that church holds several things in common with all other churches, Protestant or Roman Catholic or Orthodox. The faith of that church centers around the life, death, and resurrection of Jesus of Nazareth. That church believes some interpretation of the meaning of the life and the resurrection of Jesus. The interpretation may differ to a greater or lesser degree with what other churches teach and believe about this Galilean, but every church traces its origin back to him.

■ One procedure for each chapter suggests that your group set goals. To help you get started the study committee or leadership team might pose a question that, on the basis of study and planning, expresses the main concern of the chapter. Now as a group, ask yourselves: (1) What should we learn to help us answer this question? and (2) What should we do after we have found the answer? By your answers to these two questions, you will have set your goals for learning both content and behavior. Go through these steps as you begin the study of each new chapter, using a guiding question appropriate to the chapter.

■ A team of two persons might be prepared to define the phrase *the community of the resurrection,* as used throughout this chapter. They may begin their preparation by scanning the pages and underlining the phrase each time it appears. See also *S/R,* 3. Then by studying the setting in which it appears, they will be helped to grasp the meaning of the phrase. After their report discuss: What questions are raised in your mind about what it means for the church to be the community of the resurrection?

■ For a more detailed examination of the major issues in this chapter, use the "Chart of Key Questions" (Resource Packet, item 4). The Leaders' Guide in the packet includes instructions and questions for discussion.

Within the last century or so, a significant turning away from the Christian faith has developed. It is true that in the last decade church membership and attendance have risen to new highs. But if you read what has happened in the churches and outside them, you will discover that in the last century many new voices have challenged the central beliefs of the churches.

Our time has its share of those challenges. In this generation some of the most widely read novelists, dramatists, and poets are raising questions about the meaning of life and death. (Selected Reading [abbreviated hereafter S/R], 1.) Albert Camus is one of the best known. Other authors join him in expressing that no hope exists for man beyond this present life. They regard death as a barrier that ends the life of every creature, the highest and the lowest. Death is no gateway to the future. It is the end. What the church has called heaven and hell are conditions of life in this present world.

The church beside the street or road near you began in an age that was asking questions very similar to those persons are asking today. Does life have any meaning beyond this present moment? If not, why be so concerned about the way we live? If it does have meaning, how can its meaning be found, and what are its implications for the last half of the twentieth century? (S/R, 2.)

If we could get rid of our own understanding of the church for a few moments and go back to that spring day when Jesus, the teacher from Nazareth, was crucified, we would be very surprised that the church began at all. The records of the New Testament are clear and unanimous in telling how Jesus was deserted at the last by his disciples. One had betrayed him to the authorities and the others fled and hid behind locked doors. Peter, who had been so certain he would remain faithful to Jesus, did follow at a distance; but at the end he too denied knowing Jesus. It is one of the most remarkable events of history that those disciples who were so fearful in the first hours after the crucifixion could later become the core of the early church. How it began is told in the early chapters of the Book of Acts.

The beginning of the church and the resurrection are so closely tied that it is impossible to think of one apart from the other. Out of the faith in the resurrection arose the Christian church. And the church you attend has its roots in that first church, the community of the resurrection. (S/R, 3.)

The idea of some kind of existence of life after death was not new at the time of Jesus. Jesus and most of his contemporaries believed in a universe of three stories. The earth was the middle story; hell or the dwelling place of the dead was the lower story; and heaven was the upper story. The dwelling place of the dead was called in Hebrew "Sheol" (rhymes with *he-role*). It was located under the ground. When a group rebelled against the leadership of Moses, the ground opened up and the rebels fell alive into Sheol. (See Numbers 16:1-40, particularly verse 33.) It was a dark place, a place of silence.

By the time Jesus lived, Sheol had been transformed in the thinking of the Jews into a kind of halfway station between life on earth and resurrection. It was thought to be divided into two parts—one part where the unrighteous suffered even before the final resurrection and the other part where the righteous were rewarded. This is why, in the parable of the poor man and the rich man, Jesus pictured the poor man already in the bosom of Abraham, while the rich man suffered in Hades. (See Luke 16:19-31 for this story.) The portion of the righteous was called paradise; it was this paradise Jesus spoke of to the thief on the cross. (Luke 23:43.)

HOW OTHERS THOUGHT OF IMMORTALITY

The belief in some kind of existence after the earthly life is finished is not unique to the Hebrew people. At the very time of Jesus' life, the Greek world was greatly interested in immortality.

If you were to question every person who attends your church about his hope for life after death, you would probably receive a variety of answers. Some persons would express a deep longing for assurance of life after death. Others would say that they were satisfied with life as it can be lived here and now; they would not be especially concerned about whether or not a life exists after this one.

If you should question these same persons on how they

17

feel about dying, however, you would probably find a universal apprehension of death. Death is the great unknown. Whether or not one finds life here and now of supreme importance, the apprehension of death itself is characteristic of almost every age. The fear of utter annihilation is found even among those who outwardly express little interest in resurrection or immortality. (*S/R*, 4.)

■ Have one person read aloud the two paragraphs immediately preceding this procedure. Then poll the members of the group about their hope of life after death. How many feel the first view more nearly expresses their feelings—a deep longing for a continuation of life? How many share the second view—not especially concerned about assurance of a life after this one?

Discussion: If you hold the first view: (1) Is it that you just *long* for a continuation of life or do you *believe* in it? (2) If you believe in it, on what do you base your faith? (3) How important for this belief is your participation in the community of the resurrection?

If you are not especially concerned about assurance of life after this one: (1) Is it because you have not had it proved? (2) Or are you simply willing to trust God? (3) Or do you just avoid thinking about it? (4) Does the idea of the church as the community of the resurrection have any significance for you? What?

■ How do you feel after reading *S/R*, 4? How would you respond? Read *S/R*, 8.

The Greek-Roman world at the time of Jesus held a universal interest in religion and religious questions. Greek and, later, Roman religions were severely rationalistic. They became philosophies instead of religions. When they did, they gave up all their sacred traditions, all the symbols and myths that gave meaning to their religious practices. This religion (or philosophy, as it more properly was) lost its ability to reflect on human life, and vitality disappeared. Religion then became a process by which the principles of the science of the day were made into a theology.

These sterile religions of Greece and Rome were then replaced by a new kind of faith, called "the mystery religions." They were given that name because they were highly symbolic, appealed to the emotions rather than reason, and brought believers into a kind of secret society where central truths were given only to believers. To outsiders, they were indeed "mysteries."

How did these mystery religions take the place of the philosophical religions of Greece and Rome? The mystery religions appealed to certain aspects of life that the more reasonable religions ignored. They quenched the thirst for religious emotion, which is a universal part of man's personality. The mystery religions were *certain* of what they taught at a period of history when men deeply needed certainties.

There are some startling parallels between the character of the Greek-Roman world and our own. (1) Religious rites tended to be reproduced without change because they had been inherited from the ancestors. (2) Religious formulas were no longer understood or considered vital to the people. (3) The principles of science were adopted as the principles of theology. (4) Art lost its appeal to the common people and became a learned expression of subtle symbols. (5) Tired of searching for truth, disappointed because science had not yielded formulas for successful living, the people turned to faiths that seemed to have a consistent rule of life. (6) Morality did not respond to the demands of justice. (7) Religion became so wedded to politics that it became a means by which the ruling authority sought to control the people.

■ Note the description of the spiritual conditions existing at the time of the mystery religions, page 18. In the above paragraph, parallel conditions that exist today are given. Let groups of four persons consider one of these conditions. More than one group may deal with the same point if the class is large. Use these questions to guide you: Where or how is this condition apparent in today's society? What are the manifestations of it? If the manifestations are bad, what remedies would you suggest? What should be the response of the church?

Persons yearned for a better world. Many were satisfied with the view that good things should be enjoyed here and now, for only dust and ashes awaited them after death. Other thoughtful people were less satisfied; they turned toward these "mystery religions" in their search for redemption.

Still others found in the beliefs and practices of the young Christian church a sense of hope and purpose that made life worthwhile. The church was still young when Nero began to persecute the Christians in Rome. Rome burned (some said the fire was started by Nero himself), and Christians were charged. A few confessed that they were Christians and were arrested. Then others came forward to make the same confession. They were condemned to die in various ways. Some were crucified; some were dipped in pitch and set on fire; others were mauled and torn to pieces by wild animals. (S/R, 5.)

How could these Christians voluntarily accept this prospect of death? They did so because they were a part of the community of the resurrection. In the days of persecution, some fell away; but others remained faithful. Mutual support and the prospect of resurrection made it possible for them to withstand every torture the Romans could devise.

EAGER TO DIE

The newspapers carried accounts with pictures of Buddhists in Vietnam who committed suicide by burning themselves to death. In the United States, a man burned himself to death on the grounds of the Pentagon in Washington. Why? Because these persons (however misguided we may think them to have been) wished by their deaths to call public attention to their hope for resolving the problems facing our world. Some call it suicide; others call it martyrdom.

The early church had its martyrs, some too eager to die. One martyr of the early church was Ignatius (pronounced ig-NAY-shus). His death, early in the second century, reflects a resurrection joy in his desire to be a martyr. He was arrested in the town of Antioch in Asia Minor, where he was a bishop. On his way to Rome, while he was chained to ten soldiers, he wrote letters to various churches. Many churches along the way sent delegations to encourage him on his journey. He exhorted them to witness firmly to the love of God in Christ, whom God had resurrected from the dead. "I would rather die for Christ than rule the whole church. It is glorious to go down in the world in order to go up to God." He wanted the wild beasts to tear him to pieces and grind him to flour with their teeth that he might sooner be made into the pure bread of God.

What judgments do modern Christians make on persons like Ignatius? Our first expression is wonder. We cannot understand why a person would want to be eaten alive by wild animals. If we take these martyrs' own professions, however, we see in them a devout faith of men to whom eternal life was more precious and more real than life here on earth. For Ignatius and other martyrs, the community of the resurrection extended from this world and this life into eternity. Ignatius called the bread of the communion the "medicine of immortality," which assured him of resurrection.

DARKENED WITH SORROW

Augustine (354-430) was a famous teacher in the early church. In his book *Confessions,* which is a kind of spiritual autobiography, Augustine tells of the despair that overtook him when a young friend died. Augustine was not at that time a Christian. They had grown up together, gone to school together, and played together. When they grew to young manhood, both took up the same studies. His young friend got sick, recovered, then died a short time later.

My heart was darkened over with sorrow, and whatever I looked at was death. My own country was a torment to me, my own home was a strange unhappiness. All those things which we had done and said together became, now that he was gone, sheer torture to me. My eyes looked for him everywhere and could not find him. And as to the places where we used to meet I hated all

21

of them for not containing him; nor were they able to say to me now, "Look, he will soon come," as they used to say when he was alive and away from me. I had become a great riddle to myself and I used to ask my soul why it was sad and why it disquieted me so sorely. And my soul did not know what to answer.*

Later in life, Augustine became a Christian, a bishop, and the greatest teacher of the early church. He would later write a book on immortality. Belief in resurrection was not for him a selfish hope for continued personal existence. It was a faith that enabled one to live according to the will of God.

HELL, PURGATORY, HEAVEN

The Middle Ages have been called "the age of faith." During this period the great cathedrals of Europe were built, structures that have excited the piety and admiration of Christians in every age since that time. For nearly three hundred years, beginning in the eleventh century, these cathedrals lifted the thoughts of mankind in daily sermons. Most people could not read or write, and the stories of the Bible told in stained glass and sculpture enabled them to understand the fundamentals of the Christian faith. The lofty buildings reminded men of the hope of a life beyond.

Not all the monuments of the Middle Ages were built of stone. *The Divine Comedy* by Dante, an Italian poet, had as its subject the story of what happens to the soul after death. Dante tells the story of a visit to hell, purgatory, and heaven. On the journey, he found many famous persons of the past and of his own time. Those whose sins were worst suffered unending punishment in hell. Hell was a deep pit in the earth. Those whose sins were not as serious and therefore forgivable, whose agony was not as severe and would not last for eternity, were in purgatory. Purgatory was a mountain that began at the brink of hell. At the top of the mountain of purgatory, heaven began. Dante was led on this part of his journey to the throne of God, but its brilliance was so great that he could not see God himself.

22

Dante followed the scheme worked out in the medieval church. Hell was for those beyond hope. Purgatory was for those who could receive pardon for their sins, but who had to undergo some suffering. Heaven, or paradise, was for those already pardoned. Perhaps never before or since had mankind lived with such concern for religion as during the Middle Ages. Men feared death and the prospect of thousands of years in purgatory. When indulgences were offered—that is, when the church made it possible to shorten one's time in purgatory—thousands of people bought these for themselves and persons already dead, so that the time in purgatory might be shortened and the soul might go on to heaven. The abuses in the sale of these indulgences, the view that one could buy an indulgence without personal repentance, contributed to the demand for reform that led finally to the Protestant Reformation.

"THIS BODY THEY MAY KILL"

In many ways Martin Luther was more a medieval man than a modern one. Yet it was his work that brought about the separation from the Roman Church and the distinctive beginnings of Protestantism.

Luther's life was centered in the church. He regarded the break with Rome a tragedy when it came. Reformation within the church was his original intention. After his excommunication from the church, his views still showed deep concern for the community of the resurrection. He did not fight his battle for the sake of a churchless individualism.

Death was the great destruction of those who said "No" to God. The Christian should accept death willingly as a part of the plan of God. The law of death is a part of the gospel for the Christian. In an attitude far removed from that of the twentieth century, Luther said, "We should be happy to be dead and desire to die." * There was nothing to fear. "A Christian neither tastes nor sees death. That is, he

23

does not feel it and is not terrified by it, but goes into it calmly and peacefully as though he were going to sleep and were not really dying. A godless man, however, feels death and is eternally terrified by it. The word of God makes this difference. The Christian has this word and holds fast to it in death."*

Luther condemned selfishness among Christians in any form. Eternal life was not, for him, the mere hope that life would never end; it was for him a part of the person's relationship to Christ. This relationship must be preceded, he taught, by relationships to the church. To be a part of this community, one must accept both the gift and the task of discipleship. The person who is a member of the community of the resurrection is called to take upon himself the troubles of the church, the suffering of those who are innocent, and the needs of the poor. (S/R, 6.) Christians who thought of the church as a source of exclusive help for their own selfish needs were condemned. "They watch out for themselves, puff themselves up and never get around to being gracious to sinners. They do not even know that they should become servants and that their religiosity should serve the others." *

The community of the resurrection must take upon itself the role of servant, just as Christ did. He who desires eternal life must take upon himself the burden of Christ in life.

ONE THING HE LACKED

In the two years before his conversion in 1738, which includes the period when he was a missionary in the colony of Georgia in the New World, John Wesley was unusually concerned about death. When a severe storm threatened to sink the ship on which he was traveling to Georgia in 1736, Wesley realized shamefully that he was not prepared to die. Most of the passengers, including Wesley, were seized by panic during the storm. He noticed, however, that a group of German Moravians—men, women, and children—did not show the slightest fear of death. On his return to England early in 1738, Wesley was more fearful than before when the ship was in danger.

He soon recognized that his fear of death was a sign that he lacked faith in God. He felt he should not even be called a Christian. Praying as never before, Wesley asked God for a complete transformation of his own life. This was soon to come on May 24, 1738. (S/R, 7.)

At first glance, it seems that Wesley desired to be saved from his fear of death only for his own comfort. The story of his life after that transformation shows, however, that he did not think of his own welfare. Rather, his first impulse was for the needs of his fellow men. His interpretation of his mission was to take the gospel to those who had been forgotten by the church. Though he was often ridiculed, he found grateful listeners to his message.

Wesley had a broad view of the church. The church was "a company of men, called by the gospel, grafted into Christ by baptism, animated by love, united by all kind of fellowship." * The bands he established were a part of the church by his definition. Persons were exhorted to abstain from doing evil and to be zealous in good works. Christians are full of hope for immortality. Death is not a loss for them, for their prospect is for eternity.

■ The leadership team might have ready for distribution headlines and pictures clipped from recent newspapers. Divide the class into pairs. Each pair should have a picture or a clipping. Let these questions guide the conversation: According to your understanding of the role of the community of the resurrection, what action is called for by the headline or picture? What guidance do you get from Luther or Wesley's beliefs and examples? (See pages 23-25 and S/R, 6 and 7). Would/might your belief or non-belief in the resurrection alter your response to the clipping? How?

THE RESURRECTION AND LIFE TODAY

With the Reformation, the belief in purgatory perished for Protestants. In more recent times, hell has been banished from popular belief. Today a widespread sentimental notion has developed that all those who are dead are in heaven. Unfortunately, many contemporary funerals convey this idea instead of affirming the Christian faith.

Does the church have a realistic message to answer the claims of those who contend that nothing exists beyond this life?

Let us consider two points. First, there is a danger that any hope of eternal life may be basically self-centered. This view is contrary to the view that the purpose of the Christian faith is ultimately to turn the believer from self-interest and self-concern to God and others. It is possible to advocate a belief in immortality to perpetuate selfishness. Second, any hope of eternal life depends on our faith in God. Without faith in God, eternal life seems impossible. With faith, belief in eternal life seems certain. (S/R, 8.)

When those first disciples of Jesus felt the power of the resurrection, what was their response? The records in the New Testament do not suggest a self-centered concern about their own future lives. If the apostle Paul may be taken as an example, his belief in the resurrection sent him out on a lifetime of ministry and finally to a martyr's death. Moreover, quite likely his service to God deepened his faith in the resurrection and strengthened him to write the fifteenth chapter of First Corinthians. Undoubtedly, the resurrection of Jesus caused the Gospels to be written, including the command to proclaim salvation to the ends of the earth. The experience of the resurrection was not purely individual; it was in the community that Christ became known as the Risen One. These first witnesses to the resurrection sought to share their faith with a wider circle, and so the church began. When the credulous disciples were convinced of the resurrection, their joy knew no bounds. They could show the same kind of love to others as Christ had shown to them. This conviction was so strong that 1 John 3:14 declared, "He

26

who does not love remains in death." That conviction drew them together as the community of the resurrection.

The Christian community—the church—owes its existence to the acts of God. When Christ was raised from the dead, the church began as God's new creation for the reconciliation of the world. What called the church together? It was faith in the resurrection.

What is the church's answer to the nihilism of our time? It is the call to community, a community of worship and service. The church cannot extend a promise to mankind that becoming a member of the institutional church will overcome this pessimism. It can only say that the witness of the ages testifies that thousands have overcome such pessimism by devoting their lives to that invisible fellowship within and without the visible church dedicated to the work of Christ. Becoming a part of this fellowship is becoming a part of the community of the resurrection.

This book will try to show how this community of the resurrection has developed in the twenty centuries since Christ first appeared. The story of the church is not always a pleasant one. In some ages, the church has seemed to be on the side of evil rather than on the side of good. In the name of Christ, it has slain those who refused to conform. In other ages, the church has performed valiant service for the world. It has truly been a witness to the good news.

■ What was the response of the disciples, as a result of their experience of the resurrection? Listen as two persons read Acts 2. One person may act as narrator and the other may read Peter's statements.

Now, examine the pictures at the center of the book of selected readings entitled *We Have This Heritage*. How do they give evidence of a belief in the resurrection similar to that of the early disciples?

■ As a benediction, read silently *S/R*, 8.

■ Let the leadership team be prepared to give assignments for the next chapter of study and the members of the group be prepared to accept the assignments.

27

NOTES ON CHAPTER 1

Page 14: Albert Camus, *The Stranger,* translated by Stuart Gilbert (Vintage Books, 1946), page 1. Copyright 1946 by Alfred A. Knopf, Inc. Used by permission of Alfred A. Knopf, Inc.

Page 14: *The Stranger,* page 152. Used by permission.

Page 14: *The Stranger,* page 152. Used by permission.

Pages 21-22: *The Confessions of St. Augustine,* translated by Rex Warner. Copyright © 1963 by Rex Warner. Reprinted by arrangement with The New American Library, Inc., New York. Pages 74-75.

Page 23: Paul Althaus, *The Theology of Martin Luther,* translated by Robert C. Schultz (Fortress Press, 1966), page 408. Copyright © 1966 by Fortress Press. Used by permission.

Pages 23-24: *The Theology of Martin Luther,* page 409. Used by permission.

Page 24: *The Theology of Martin Luther,* page 309. Used by permission.

Page 25: John Wesley, *Explanatory Notes Upon the New Testament,* Acts 5:11.

Read these selections in your Bible:
Psalms 8:1-9
God's majesty and man's crown.

1 Timothy 4:1-16
"Everything created by God is good."

1 Peter 4:12-19
Born anew in Christ.

2

□□□

LEAVE IT?—ACCEPT IT?
—CHANGE IT?

"I am *sick*. I am sick of everything in this hot, stupid, fly-ridden *world*. . . . I am sick of going to bed and I am sick of waking up. . . . I am tired . . . I am tired of the truth . . . and I am tired of lying about the truth . . . I am tired of my skin. . . . I WANT OUT! *

These are the feelings expressed by a nurse in Edward Albee's play, *The Death of Bessie Smith*. The play is based on the death of a Negro blues singer who bled to death after an automobile accident in 1937 because the white hospitals refused to give her medical aid.

Evil and suffering are rampant in this world. (*S/R*, 9.) Murder, robbery, prejudice, and hate fill the pages of our newspapers. All over the world children go hungry, even in America. Cancer, smallpox, and other deadly diseases take their daily tolls. The cost of war in property and lives, both

---

■ *As you arrive at your place of meeting, check the assignment chart for specific preparation to be made before the session begins.*
■ *Set goals for your study of this chapter as suggested on page 15.*

military and civilian, is frightfully staggering. Even worse is the maiming and killing of thousands of people in automobile accidents in the United States.

In view of such suffering and evil, many Christians have denied the goodness of the world and have attempted in various ways to escape from it. This kind of Christianity almost always focuses on otherworldliness. It is a common reaction to suffering and heavy burdens.

On the other hand, many Christians have accepted God's creation of the world and his activity in it as good. They have tried to identify with the world. This kind of Christianity almost always accommodates itself—adjusts itself—to the world and its ways.

Other Christians have affirmed the world and attempted to transform it. This kind of Christianity almost always sees the tension between what the world is and what Christ taught. They want to see the spirit and message of Christ applied to the world, to correct its evils as far as possible, and to help persons find a better life, both spiritual and material. Variations of the social gospel represent the efforts to apply the message of Christ to the problems of mankind. Religious leaders who are trying to solve the problems caused by racial tension in the United States are examples today. They do not reject the world; they want to transform its injustices. (S/R, 10.)

These three ways of looking at the world—(1) the wish to escape from it, (2) acceptance of it, or (3) the affirmation of it and the hope to transform it—have often been found in the church's history. Sometimes all three are mixed.

"Is this world good?" is not an idle question. Every generation, every individual faces it in some form.

■ Why study church history? Listen while two persons discuss the question by reading aloud "Why Study Church History?" (Resource Packet, item, 2). The Leaders' Guide in the packet includes instructions and questions to be discussed after the conversation.

■ Read silently the preceding sections. Note especially the three ways of looking at the world. Then let a member of the leadership team display the picture "Barbed Wire" (Resource Packet, item 7). As the picture is being studied, one person might read aloud *S/R*, 9.

Now, let each person write, on paper or a 3x5 card, his answers to these questions: What questions are raised in your mind by the picture, the preceding paragraphs, and the selected reading? (The Leaders' Guide in the packet includes additional questions.) When you feel about the world as the nurse quoted at the beginning of this chapter did, how do you express it? What questions do you ask? What ways, other than death, are used by some to escape the world? Which of the three ways of looking at the world seems most appropriate at this point in your study? At the end of the session, look again at what you have written. Have you changed your opinions? Why? Why not?

PERSECUTIONS

Golgotha reminds us of what this world can do. From the stoning of Stephen (Acts 7) to the beginning of the fourth century, Christians suffered. They were flogged, pitted against lions, stoned, nailed on crosses, and burned alive. They became an underground, secret society.

In Romans 13 Paul urges all Christians to obey whoever is ruling "for he is God's servant for your good." Since all authority is from God, Christians obey God when they obey authorities, writes Paul. First Peter shows that the Christians believed their lot would be improved if they gave no occasion for complaint (2:12-15; 3:16; 4:12-13). By the time John wrote his Revelation, the Christians had come to associate the rulers with Satanic powers. From beneath the throne of God, the slain martyrs cry out for revenge, "O Sovereign Lord, holy and true, how long before thou wilt judge and avenge our blood on those who dwell upon the earth?" (See Revelation 6:9-11; 20:1-3.)

Between the time of Paul and the writer of the Book of Revelation, a great change had come in the attitude of the Christians toward worldly authorities. Nero blamed them for the fire in Rome in A.D. 64. Two ancient writers, Tacitus

31

(pronounced *TASS-i-tus*) and Suetonius (pronounced *swe-TONE-i-us*), tell about the ordeals that the Christians suffered. Domitian (pronounced *doe-MISH-un*), emperor from 81 to 96, launched a persecution. He seized the Christians' property and exiled or condemned to death hundreds of Christians for "crimes" against the state. They were accused of causing storms, bad business, and illness!

Despite all this, Christianity spread. In 303 the emperor Diocletian (*die-o-KLEE-shun*) faced the decision of whether to make the Christians his allies or to exterminate them. He chose the latter. His persecution, the last great one, exceeded all the others in cruelty, terror, and passion. He ordered that churches be destroyed, Bibles burned, Christians deprived of public office and civil rights, and that everyone sacrifice to the pagan gods or die.

A few years later Constantine (*KONN-stan-TEEN*) — who ruled in Gaul, Britain, and Spain—chose the Christians as allies and crossed over the Alps with his conquering army under a sign of Christ. He established himself as emperor and granted the Christians legal toleration in 313. He also ordered that Christian property be restored to the Christians at imperial expense. Under Theodosius (*the-o-DOE-shus*) the Great (379-395) Christianity became the *only* legal religion in the empire.

The martyrs bore a glorious witness to the good news. This must not be taken from them. But they also fostered an otherworldliness that devalued living and working in the world now. Though not without exceptions, they wanted to forsake the world. They longed for heaven.

ISOLATION FROM THE WORLD

How deep this rejection of the world was in the early church may be seen in the fact that when the persecutions stopped, many Christians still continued to reject the world. With the edict of Constantine, its membership increased. Overnight the church became a status symbol.

When "the world" poured into the church, those who longed to live disciplined, ascetic lives left. These were laymen. In the fourth century they began leaving the church by the thousands. They went to caves in the hills, to old tombs in deserted graveyards, and to the waste places of the desert.

These monks thought that they had a better chance for salvation by leaving sinful society, denying themselves, and living away from other men and women. They ate as little as possible, went months and years without bathing, slept in uncomfortable positions, wore only enough clothing for decency, and shunned sex. They neglected the body, believing that material things and the body in particular were evil. Little sleep and extreme fasting helped weaken the body so that sex would not tempt them. (*S/R,* 11.)

One of the most famous of the monks was Simeon Stylites (*SIM-e-on STY-li-tees*). He retreated from the world by sitting on top of a column that was first twelve, then twenty-two, and finally forty cubits high—roughly sixty feet. The top of the column measured only a yard wide. He began his column-sitting in 423 and stayed there for thirty-six years without coming down once. Food was hauled up by a rope. His major preoccupation was preaching against the evils of this life.

Gradually a change took place in monasticism. Instead of living alone, monks began to live in groups. The monks realized that they could not completely isolate themselves. During the Dark Ages of the barbarian conquests, when the lights of Western culture grew dim, the monks maintained libraries, hostels, hospitals, orphanages, and schools. In spite of their basic rejection of the world, the monks became the means by which culture and Christianity survived.

WORLD REJECTION IN AMERICA

The right to freedom of worship, written into the American Constitution, has never been illustrated better than the

33

period before 1850. Religions arose, prospered, and declined. There was a restlessness, a search for something unknown that seemed to be missing from life. This search resulted in the popularity of some unusual religious groups. One of these was the Millerite movement, out of which has come the Seventh-Day Adventists and other adventist groups.

The Millerite movement got its name from William Miller, who lived in Vermont. On the basis of his study of prophecies in the Bible, he became convinced that Christ would return to earth in the year 1843. For several years before this time, Miller checked and rechecked his figures to be sure of the date. In the year 1828 he made his first announcement of the Second Coming.

Miller's reputation spread in the 1830's. He held huge camp meetings and vividly described what that last day would be like. Thousands were turned away from these meetings. Popular excitement rose to fever pitch during the late 1830's and early 1840's. As the year 1843 approached, more and more converts came over to his beliefs. Miller himself tried to calm the people. He was not exactly sure when the last day would come, but some of the Millerite preachers threw caution to the wind and announced the exact day. When the end of 1843 approached, the tension mounted. Merchants gave away their goods because soon there would be no use for them. Fear of the last judgment caused many to commit suicide. Others were driven insane by the waiting. One man, clad in white robes, climbed a tree on the appointed day. When he thought the hour was near, he tried to fly, fell, and broke his neck.

A new date was set: October 22, 1844. Excitement renewed. Voting was light in elections because the end was at hand. Some sold all they had to pay their debts and to help pay the debts of other believers who wanted to enter the new age with a clean slate. Business was neglected.

On the night of October 21, these people assembled to await the great moment. No food was brought, for none would be needed. The night passed, the next day, the next night. There were many suicides from the strain, and again others were led away insane. Heartbroken, the Millerites returned to their homes they had neglected and to crops that had remained unharvested.

Another religious faith native to America is Christian Science. It also rejects the world and all matter. Begun by Mrs. Mary Baker Eddy, the first Christian Science church was established in Boston in 1879. According to this faith, the only reality is in God and what he creates. Whatever is contrary to God is unreal. Faithful to the view of its founder, Christian Science rejects matter—the world of the physical senses—as unreal. Evil is unreal; sin lasts only as long as *belief* in sin lasts. Disease, for instance, is unreal; it is in the mind and when spiritual truth is introduced, disease leaves. (*S/R*, 12.)

The Amish faith is a group who rejects the modern world. They do not use automobiles or electricity; they use hooks and eyes on their clothes instead of buttons or zippers, and worship in private homes. In recent years, they have been in the news because of their opposition to the public schools. They have their own schools and feel their children will be contaminated if they are required to attend school with non-Amish children. The Amish men wear broad hats and do not shave after marriage. Women wear the dress of a century ago. They travel in horse-drawn buggies and wagons. For the sake of the purity of their religious faith, they wish to keep to themselves and avoid the temptations of modern life.

■ Have a symposium panel (persons give prepared remarks) present and discuss attempts at and reasons for world rejection by various religious groups. Each member of the panel will make a brief presentation about one of the following:

1. Martyrs and world rejection
2. Monastics and world rejection
3. Millerites and world rejection
4. Amish and world rejection

5. World rejection evidenced in gospel songs such as: "On Jordan's Stormy Banks I Stand," "Dwelling in Beulah Land," and "This World Is Not My Home."

Use the material provided on pages 31-35 and in the suggested selected readings as a basis for the presentations. Examine the gospel songs suggested to determine where and how they speak of world rejection. It might be interesting to compare the attitude toward the world seen in the gospel songs with that in "This Is My Father's World" (*The Methodist Hymnal*, 45).

Let the symposium begin with the reading of 1 Timothy 4:1-5. Then after the five presentations, divide the class into groups of four to six persons. Let each group analyze *one* of the five views by using these questions: What do these groups think is accomplished through their rejection? How has this rejection helped or hindered their witness to the good news?

■ Have one member of the class be prepared to compare the world rejection discussed above with the withdrawal from society of non-church groups like the Hippies, motorcycle gangs like Hell's Angels, or the drug culture. What similarities or differences are seen in their motivation?

Discuss in the total group: Some Christians in all ages have felt that in order to maintain the purity of their faith and to avoid the temptations of modern life they must refuse to conform to the normal patterns of life in the world. Why don't *all* Christians? How does one decide what to reject? How does one decide what style of life to live?

■ Form work groups of four to six persons. Have each group select one of the following areas about which they will ask the question, How has the attitude of the church in the past influenced our views and actions in relation to this area?

A. Attitude toward money—a necessary evil
B. Standards of success—Christians should not seek success
C. Participation in politics—stick to the "simple gospel"
D. Attitude toward the arts—strange people with strange ideas
E. Sex education—hush, hush
F. Separation of business and religion—nice guys finish last

What kinds of problems arise as a result of these attitudes? What does world affirmation suggest about ways to solve these problems? If time permits, let one person from each group briefly share the ideas of the group.

ACCOMMODATION TO THE WORLD

Did the whole church in the Middle Ages withdraw from the world? No. The main body of the church tried to live in the belief that the world was of secondary importance. At the same time, the church tried to accommodate itself to the world. That is, it was not critical of the world. Sometimes it even accepted the standards of the world rather than the standards of Christ. "To accommodate" means to adjust to the circumstances or to favor. Accommodation meant to favor the powers of the world rather than God.

During the Middle Ages (500-1500) the popes sought and achieved domination of western Europe. How could the church have so much power? Because men longed for release from the hardships of medieval life, their hope of getting to heaven was strong and vivid. Many monks, nuns, and mystics disdained life in the flesh. They regarded spiritual matters as the only ones worth bothering about. Poverty, chastity, and obedience were the primary vows of the great new religious orders, such as the Franciscans, founded by St. Francis. St. Francis said his followers could own nothing, not even a psalter. They willingly gave away their clothes if someone asked for them. They punished their bodies by wearing hair shirts. They refused to store up food. Yet St. Francis served others in any way he could and gloried in the good creation of God. Later, the order he founded gave in to worldly standards.

St. Francis did not try to transform the world. He strictly enjoined obedience to the local priests, no matter how corrupt they might be. Even though all the religious orders did not live up to their vows—even his became wealthy—their total impact pointed to this life in the world as secondary.

The medieval church saw no radical separation between its otherworldly and this-worldly emphases. Society was not something to reform or convert. The church and state were partners, filtering down the dictates of God to the people, assuring salvation through the sacraments and obedience.

ACCOMMODATION IN AMERICA

The best examples of accommodation of the church to the world in American church life occurred in the 1800's.

Since the church exercised a place of prominent leadership in the early days of the thirteen colonies, there was little question of accommodation during the early years of the American church.

The two most widespread revival movements in America took place in the 1700's. The first, in the 1740's; the second, in the 1790's, continuing into the 1800's. These revivals emphasized conversion on the basis of a personal religious experience. If a person "accepted Christ"—usually a violent emotional experience—he was regarded as a Christian. He was expected to live a virtuous life thereafter. This life usually meant keeping the Ten Commandments, avoiding showy clothes and jewelry, attendance at plays or other entertainments of that kind, dancing, card-playing, drinking hard liquor, and the like.

The attitude of the churches in the 1800's toward slavery is an example of the adjustment to the world. Hardly anyone defends slavery now; but at one time, the churches were one of the forward walls in its defense. Slavery was here; those in places of responsibility felt it had to be justified. They went to the Bible and dug up every text they could find on slavery. They said Jesus had not condemned slavery. They said Paul had counseled slaves to be obedient to their masters. Neither Paul nor Jesus had said slaves should be freed. Many churches defended slavery. Such a belief split many denominations, among them the Methodist.

In the middle and last half of the 1800's, the industrial revolution began to take hold in America. Factories were enlarged. People moved from the farms into the cities to work in the factories. People by the hundreds of thousands came from foreign countries to America. These immigrants settled in the cities. The cities were then faced with the problems the like of which they had never seen before. Slums and tenements in cities were the homes of millions of people. People were thrown out of work. Bad conditions became intolerable.

At the same time, financial tycoons were building fortunes. Great monopolies were formed. John D. Rockefeller and men like him were making millions. Frequently these tycoons had little interest in the people who worked for them. In one city, for instance, a few blocks from where people were starving to death, one tycoon's wife walked her dog, which wore a collar worth $15,000. Little children went without food or medical attention and a few blocks away persons attending parties given by these tycoons lighted cigarettes with $100 bills. (S/R, 13.)

What has this to do with the church? Simply this. The church was so frequently allied with these tycoons and the upper and middle classes that it lost sight of interest in the workingman and the poor. In some textile mills, small children tended looms for fourteen hours a day. They became so tired that they sometimes fell into the machinery and were mangled.

What did the churches have to say about these conditions? In most cases, nothing. The man who owned the mill was not troubled by his conscience. He had had a personal conversion experience. He did not think his religion had anything to do with the way he ran his business. The minister of the church was afraid to be critical lest he lose the financial support of the middle and upper class. Denominational leaders seemed to have nothing to say about the great wrongs that were taking place among the poor. By their attitude, they seemed to be saying, "It's not our problem." They had forgotten the parable of the Good Samaritan. (S/R, 14.)

The last half of the 1800's is one of the most disgraceful in the history of the church. The churches were silent when they should have remembered that the prophet Amos had condemned those who lived in fine houses and ground down the faces of the poor. (S/R, 15.)

The church had accommodated to the culture. It could not bring itself to be critical. The example of Christ had been repressed. It was a blot on the history of the church which has not yet been fully erased.

How can the church tell when it is obedient to the world rather than to God? When the church is more concerned with numbers than with the quality of church life, when the church does not speak out because its message may be unpopular, when the church takes its message from the powerful and the rich, when the church is more concerned about raising money than in obedience to the concerns of Christ, it is accommodating itself to the world. It is a time of the shame of the church. (S/R, 16.)

■ Listen as two persons read aloud a modern-day version of the story of the Good Samaritan (S/R, 14). Then let the reading and the discussion of S/R, 13, 15, and 16 set the stage for discussing the accommodation of the church to the world. You might proceed in this fashion. Let groups of three persons be prepared to read and discuss the selected readings before the class. Each group may follow these steps: (1) one person will read aloud one selected reading; (2) the other two members of the team will listen and be ready to respond with their thoughts and questions. Try to limit consideration of each reading to five minutes.

Now, let the class consider some of these questions in open discussion: What reasons do I give for bypassing the needs of persons around me? How do I hurt myself when I deny my responsibility for my neighbor and brother? Is accommodation to the culture necessary and valuable? How? Why do some church members feel that the church has no responsibility to change society? Why do some want the church to defend the status quo? Why do some think the church should uphold status and privilege? If the church as an institution takes no action to relieve the oppressed, who is finally responsible?

AFFIRMATION AND TRANSFORMATION

What has been the result of Christianity in affirming the world as good and attempting to transform it? There is space here only to suggest what has happened. It should be pointed out that the early church had no design for a transformation of the world.

From its very early days, Christians insisted on monogamy. They condemned the killing by exposure of unwanted children. They criticized the amusements of the Roman Empire and played some part in eradication of the combat of gladiators. Burial customs were revised in light of the Christian belief in eternal life. Especially under the emperor Constantine, legislation was enacted to help the poor, widows, and orphans; to strengthen marriage; to encourage more humane treatment of slaves. Perhaps as important as any other change brought about in the ancient world as a result of Christianity was that a life of simplicity and dignity gained respectability: modesty in dress, eating simple foods, avoidance of intemperance in any way, a life devoted to love and service of others.

The Middle Ages (500-1500) have been called the "age of uncertainty" as well as the "age of faith." During this period the Christian faith was often weak. Yet the effects of Christianity on the world are important. Infanticide was condemned even more severely than before and many foundling hospitals were established. As Christian missionaries spread out toward northern and central Europe, both marriage and funeral customs were harmonized with Christian belief. The church cared for the orphaned, the sick, and the aged. Schools were conducted under the auspices of the church. Special attention was given those suffering from leprosy, one of the most dreaded of all diseases. The economic inequalities of society, with wealth and ease for the few and hard labor for the many, were subject to influence by the church and the cause of a more charitable attitude toward the poor. The church assisted in political unification, promoted peace (special days were set aside on which battles were not allowed), condemned feuds and tournaments, gave dignity to common labor, left its stamp on the art and literature.

It should be remembered that the church of the Middle Ages had no more program for the transformation of society than did the church of the first five centuries. It is clear, however, that even in periods when the church seemed to be rejecting the world and many Christians sought to isolate themselves from it, transformation was taking place.

What about the period since the Protestant Reformation?

Society was transformed by the new principle of religious toleration and, with the conclusion of the Thirty Years' War (1618-48), wars over religion ended. In this post-Reformation period, the first thoughts of an ideal society were put forth by men like Thomas More and James Harrington. The idea of a modern democracy grew out of the belief in the individual; Calvinism and other forms of Protestantism brought about a political revolution in Great Britain. The Christian impulse was significant in the development of international law as a means of settling disputes rather than by war. Women were given new dignity by groups like the Quakers who accorded full rights of religious participation to them. Especially Calvinism reinforced the rising capitalism in this period. Christianity had great impact on the literature of the time, especially in the King James translation of the Bible (1611) and the writings of men like John Milton. The church had a great part in the rise of popular education through the Sunday school, begun in 1783 by Robert Raikes to teach the poor, and John Wesley, who distributed inexpensive literature to the masses.

IN AMERICA

The best example of affirmation and transformation of the world by the church in the United States was through the social gospel movement. It began in the last years of the 1800's and continued up through the period of World War I. Its best-known advocates were Walter Rauschenbusch (pronounced *ROW-shen-BUSH*), Washington Gladden—both ministers—and Richard T. Ely, a layman who taught at Johns Hopkins University and the University of Wisconsin.

Those who worked in this movement had in common the belief that the church should work to improve the conditions in society, especially in the cities, that were destructive of life and its meaning. These were men who wanted to see the kingdom of God established in American life and who worked to make society conform to this ideal. They were especially concerned about living conditions in the crowded cities; about working conditions, especially where women and children were concerned; about educational opportunities for all; about improvement of sanitation and public health; and about ways of caring for the sick, the injured, the unemployed, and the elderly. The social gospel was closely related to the Progressive movement in both major political parties and worked for the social legislation enacted finally in the terms of Woodrow Wilson and Franklin Delano Roosevelt. The Social Creed of the churches came out of the social gospel era. The movement declined during the time of World War I.

In our own time, there are some striking affirmations of the world and attempts to transform it. The old optimism that the kingdom of God could be established in this world has been dimmed by two world wars and other upheavals. Many Christians, however, feel that the gospel must be put into effect in the world. One significant example is the East Harlem Protestant Parish, where a group of ministers and laymen have lived in a deprived community to work with its people for a better life. (S/R, 17.)

Some contemporary theologians think the church must more and more turn itself away from thought of any world beyond to the needs of this world. They look for a new revelation of God in the metropolis.

For the future, what shall the church's attitude be toward the world: rejection and isolation, acceptance and accommodation, or affirmation and transformation?

■ Brainstorm (spontaneous offering of ideas) possible solutions to this question: How can the church (a) encourage and support persons to follow the leading of their faith in their business, or in their social life, or in their political decisions and (b) increase opportunities for lay persons to use *all* of their talents and training (as a housewife, a businessman, a nurse, a carpenter, a psychologist, an electrician, an accountant, a cook, a teacher, and the like) to strengthen the church's ministries in the world? How would freedoms achieved through these steps help us to affirm the world?

43

■ "Chart of Key Questions" (Resource Packet, item 4) is a helpful guide to the study of the main questions in this chapter. Consult the Leaders' Guide in the packet for specific directions.

■ One person might summarize briefly the attitudes within the church toward world affirmation and transformation (pages 40-43).

Now, examine some hymns for clues to the Christian's responsibility in affirming and transforming the world. See *The Methodist Hymnal* for "Rise Up, O Men of God," 174; "The Voice of God Is Calling," 200; "Where Cross the Crowded Ways of Life," 204. You might choose one hymn for the entire group to read and discuss or let small groups discuss one of the hymns.

■ Go back and answer the final questions in the procedure at the top of page 31.

■ Select one of the hymns to sing as a benediction.

■ Let the leadership team be prepared to give assignments for the next chapter of study and the members of the group be prepared to accept the assignments.

NOTES ON CHAPTER 2

Page 29: Edward Albee, *The Zoo Story, The Death of Bessie Smith, The Sandbox* (Coward-McCann, 1960), pages 124-25. Copyright © 1960 by Edward Albee. Used by permission of the publisher.

Read these selections in your Bible:
Mark 4:35-41
"Who then is this?"

Matthew 16:13-23
"You are the Christ."

John 10:22-33
"I and the Father are one."

Mark 10:35-45
A ransom for many.

3

□□□
WHY FOLLOW CHRIST?

Why not follow Buddha, Confucius, Socrates, or Billy Graham?

Is Christ God? Is he man? Can we *imitate* Christ?

In the life of the church, how a person answered these questions could be the difference between life and death. Stephen was stoned because he said Christ was the Righteous One, the Son of man (Acts 7). Thousands of martyrs in the early years of the church died because they called Christ Lord and King. Peter Waldo said Mary was the mother of Jesus. The church held that she was the mother of God. Therefore, Peter Waldo was not allowed to preach. In north Italy and in France, his followers were killed without mercy.

In 1553, a man named Servetus (pronounced *ser-VEE-tus*) was burned by the followers of John Calvin because he denied that there were three persons in the Trinity. Some

■ *As you arrive at your place of meeting, check the assignment chart for specific preparation to be made before the session begins.*
■ *Set goals for your study of this chapter as suggested on page 15.*

45

Baptists were burned by Queen Elizabeth I in 1575 because they said Christ was less than God. King James I, for whom the King James Version of the Holy Bible is named, sentenced two men to be burned in 1612 because they were uncertain that Christ was equal to God.

■ Check the statement that comes closest to expressing what you believe about Jesus.

___ (1) I believe Jesus was God.

___ (2) I believe Jesus was the Son of God.

___ (3) I believe Jesus was a good and holy man who did all that is attributed to him in the New Testament.

___ (4) I believe Jesus was a good man, but the accounts of his miraculous deeds are not to be taken literally.

___ (5) None of the above represents what I believe. What I believe about Jesus is _____.

■ Use the "Chart of Key Questions" (Resource Packet, item 4) to guide your group in considering the major questions in this session. Consult the Leaders' Guide in the packet.

WHO IS CHRIST?

Who is Christ that we should follow him? Was he a great prophet? a great teacher? a divine-human person? Even the New Testament is not entirely clear on all these points. The writers of the New Testament obviously intended to convince their readers that Jesus was the Messiah. But the Jews living in the time expected the Messiah to be a worldly ruler. In the Gospel of Mark, Jesus seems in the early period of his ministry to want to keep a secret from his followers that he is the Messiah. (Mark 4:41; 6:45-52; 7:37; 8:16-21, 27-33; 9:32.) The faithfulness of the disciples was tested the night Jesus was betrayed. Not only did Judas desert him but also those who had been closest to him during his ministry. The common people who had earlier followed him with such interest now fell away and called for his death.

These actions just described do not appear to be the actions of people who really believed that Jesus was the Christ.

When Peter says Jesus is the Christ, Jesus charges Peter

46

and the other disciples to tell no one about him. (Mark 8: 29-30.) When Jesus asks questions about who he is, he suggests that he himself had not yet made clear to his own disciples his identity. (Matthew 16:13-23; Luke 9:18-22.) At his trial Jesus admitted he was the Christ. (Mark 14: 61 and following.) According to Matthew and Luke he did not give a direct answer to the question of the high priests.

It is clear that Jesus was not the kind of Messiah that most of the Jews had expected. They had hoped for a messianic Son of David who would restore their nation to its past glory. The New Testament tells of a mother who came to Jesus with her sons and asked that one son might sit on the right hand and one on the left hand in the kingdom of Jesus. (Matthew 20:20-27.) This episode indicates that many thought Jesus was establishing a kingdom on earth.

The crucifixion and resurrection changed completely the ideas of many people about the nature of the kingdom of God. Christ was no longer looked upon as an earthly king but as the Exalted Lord. God had shown his approval of his Son by raising him from the dead. More than any other thing, belief in the resurrected Christ distinguished the early Christians from the Jews.

The victory over death was so important to the early Christians that they began to worship on the day of the Resurrection—the first day of the week, which we call Sunday.

The skeptical Jews very early began to accuse the Christians of having two gods. Christians themselves were forced to explain in what sense Jesus was a man and in what sense he was God. These controversies over exactly who Jesus was, his relationship to God and the implications of these ideas took a great deal of the time and energy of the church for the first three centuries. (S/R, 18.)

WAS CHRIST LESS THAN GOD?

Was the Son created like everything and everyone else?

47

Did God really come to earth in Christ? Was Jesus the Christ even before the beginning of time?

Questions like these began the first big controversy in the early church. A man by the name of Arius (pronounced *AIR-e-us*) stirred the controversy to white heat.

Constantine was the new emperor of the Roman Empire. He had stopped persecuting Christians as his predecessors had done, and he eventually gave them preferred status in the empire. It became an advantage to be a Christian if one wanted to get a government post or become an officer in the army. Constantine's empire was badly divided, and he needed some means to bring it together. He chose the Christian church as that means.

A storm broke out into the open about the year 320 when Arius and his bishop had a bitter quarrel on the nature of Christ. Arius insisted that Christ was created by God, that he had *not* existed from all eternity. He was not equally God in essence or eternality. Christ had a beginning; God did not.

What happened at the Incarnation? According to Arius, the spiritual Christ simply entered the man Jesus.

Arius' bishop had just the opposite view. He said that Christ was divine just like God.

This argument began in Egypt, and it involved mainly Christians living around the northern, eastern, and southern borders of the Mediterranean Sea.

Constantine, the emperor, became concerned and involved. He had hoped the church would unify his enormous empire and now a split was developing in the church. If something were not done, his empire might be split apart over religious differences. To settle the argument, Constantine called a meeting at the town of Nicaea (pronounced *ny-SEE-ah*) in 325 in the land that is modern Turkey. About three hundred bishops came, their expenses paid by the emperor.

After lengthy discussions, the bishops held a vote on what

they believed about Christ. Arius lost. The bishops agreed that Christ was not simply *like* the Father; he was the same in essence as the Father. The latter view was sponsored by the bishop with whom Arius had his quarrel.

The question of the nature of Christ was not settled once and for all. The argument continued for another fifty-six years. It was settled temporarily, only to break out again and continue for seventy more years. Today in the church persons still ask the same questions that were asked at the Council of Nicaea in 325. As the argument continued, a man by the name of Athanasius (pronounced *ATH-a-NAY-si-us*) took up the dispute. The religious problem was closely connected with the political situation. After Constantine died, the rulers switched from one side to the other.

The dispute was temporarily settled in 381 when a council met at Constantinople. By this time both Arius and Athanasius had died. The decision of that council is found today in what we know as the Nicene Creed.

Soon the controversy commenced again. Not until the year 451 was the issue finally settled in the early church.

When a person living in the twentieth century looks at an argument like this, it may seem foolish and irrelevant. Perhaps we do not use the same language as did these early churchmen to discuss our understanding of the nature of Christ. Before we can make a judgment on the past, we must have an understanding of the stakes that were involved.

Both in politics and religion there was a great deal to be gained or lost over this argument. On the side of politics, the unity of the Roman Empire was at stake.

For religion, the stakes were far more important. If Christ was not truly a man, then his victory over death seemed to have little meaning for human beings. His death had been only an *appearance*, if he was not truly man.

On the other hand, if Christ was not truly divine, then what he said of life beyond this present world could have little meaning. Only one who was truly divine could make man himself divine in the sense of giving him eternal life.

We see, therefore, that the early church felt it had to accept both these understandings of the nature of Christ—that is, that he was both human and divine—since both of them had important values for all Christians.

CHRIST AS MAN

How can the Father, Son, and Holy Spirit be the same, yet different? How can Christ be fully human and also fully divine? (S/R, 19.)

Questions like these are a stumbling block to persons today. Jesus as a man seems to get lost in discussions of whether he was human and divine.

Earlier in this chapter, Michael Servetus was mentioned. He lived in the sixteenth century. He objected strongly to speaking of the Trinity in abstract language. Servetus had read the Bible through, but he could not find the Trinity.

Servetus felt that men must recover the simplicity of the Bible itself. There is only one God. What we call Father, Son, and Holy Spirit are *dispositions* of God. Christ was an actual historical man; he was God making himself visible. In creation, God makes himself known through his works. The Holy Spirit is God making himself active in us. The Trinity is not three separate persons. The cross proved Christ was human, and the resurrection proved Christ was divine. The views of Servetus were not extremely radical, but his attack on the abstract understanding of the Trinity stirred others to go farther.

The belief against the Trinity culminated in the religion we know as the Unitarian Church. In 1774, the first Unitarian Church in the world was founded in London. In 1785, the oldest Episcopal Church in New England—King's Chapel in Boston—became the first Unitarian Church in America.

With the continued rise of science and man's increased dependence on reason, scholars such as David F. Strauss (pronounced *strouse*) and Ernest Renan (pronounced *re-*

NAN) further emphasized the humanity of Jesus. As far as they were concerned, the divinity of Jesus bordered on superstition. To Strauss and Renan, Jesus was simply a man. In his *Life of Jesus,* written in 1863, Renan carefully omitted all miracles and other details of the life of Jesus that showed him as different from an ordinary human being. There were no miracles, no virgin birth, no resurrection.

Interest in Jesus as a man continues down to our own time. In the 1920's, Bruce Barton—a successful advertising man —wrote a book about Jesus entitled *The Man Nobody Knows.* Jesus is pictured as a successful executive, an outdoor man, the sociable type, the founder of modern business. "Wist ye not that I must be about my Father's *business"* gave him the clue. With twelve unexceptional men, Jesus established a business that has been going strong for almost two thousand years. He was a thinker, a doer, a leader. He was not a weakling, a man of sorrows, or uninspiring, glad to die. He was a man! "Never explain; never retract; never apologize; get it done and let them howl," * might well have been Jesus' motto, wrote Barton. Jesus was like David Lloyd George, Abraham Lincoln, Henry Ford, and J. P. Morgan! Barton's picture of Christ was a reflection of his own ideals.

■ Discuss in the total group: In light of your own understanding of Christ, evaluate what the writer of this book feels to be essential beliefs. See also *S/R,* 19. How do you feel when persons differ with each other on their essential beliefs about Christ? How can members of the group support one another during the process of evaluating a view?

■ Role play (spontaneous acting out) a situation where one person tries to explain to another his understanding of Christ. Let the members of the class evaluate his explanation in the light of their understanding of Christ.

■ Working in pairs or as a total group, compare the views of Christ set forth in the creed of a community church and in the Apostles' Creed. (See *S/R,* 18.) Discuss: How are they similar? How do they differ? The creed of the community church is described as a "definition of religion-in-general." What is meant by that? Do you agree? Which creed more nearly states your beliefs? Why? What questions are raised in your mind by either creed?

ATONEMENT

How did Christ bring about a new relationship to God? Did he do it as a man? If so, can we achieve what he achieved? Did he do it as a divine being so that we are dependent on him and cannot be saved other than by special belief in him?

To use a modern comparison, the early church believed that man had been "kidnapped" by the devil. When a person is kidnapped, the kidnapper holds him for a ransom—a price that will be paid for his return. The apostle Paul and the Gospel of Mark both set forth the belief that sinful men had been kidnapped by the devil and the blood (meaning *life*) was required by the devil as a ransom so that men might be returned to God. (See 1 Corinthians 6:20 and Mark 10: 45.) This is called the "ransom theory" of the atonement.

Another view was called the "satisfaction theory." This view was developed in the Middle Ages by Anselm. He thought that Christ had made satisfaction to God, not to the devil. Man's sin had injured God's honor, and God demanded satisfaction. But man, being so much less than God, could not make it right. So God sent Christ to do the job, and those who are "in Christ" are released from making satisfaction.

Martin Luther, the founder of Protestantism, did not shake off the older views of the atonement. For Luther, Christ took upon himself the sins of the world. Though Christ was sinless, he took the punishment that should have been given to the blasphemer, the robber, the murderer, and the adulterer. (*S/R*, 20.) Christ became "a curse for us" (see Galatians 3:13), and since the penalty of sin cannot be extracted from both us and Christ, we are free.

These views do not satisfy those who regarded Christ as an example for man to imitate. Men long to be like Jesus.

Does God demand satisfaction? In the Middle Ages, Abelard objected to the view of Anselm. In Christ, God showed his supreme love for man. That love awakens love in us, said Abelard. The *Imitation of Christ* made so popular by

52

Thomas à Kempis had a similar basis in the life of Christ. Something about the life of Christ seems to cut through dry doctrines and appeal directly to ordinary men.

One of the most popular books ever published in America was *In His Steps* by Charles M. Sheldon. When this book came out in 1897, it created a sensation. "What would Jesus do?" was the question Christians seriously pondered as they thought about how a Christian should face problems at the beginning of the twentieth century. If he were a newspaper editor, would he report prize fights and accept liquor ads? If he had an outstanding musical voice, would he perform with a national comic opera troupe or would he sing hymns at a revival tent? If he had a million dollars, how would he invest it? In the book, the minister, Henry Maxwell, asked members of his congregation to pledge themselves for a whole year "to obey Jesus' teachings and follow in his steps regardless of what others might do." Life in the small city changed dramatically. Do many Christians today, when faced with a difficult decision, ask themselves, "What would Jesus do?" (*S/R*, 21.)

■ Let groups of four or five persons discuss one of the views of the atonement (pages 52-53). What is the central idea about Christ in this view? How does this view threaten or support my own view? How can this view help me to accept differences in thought about the atonement?

CONCLUSIONS

In our time, in the twentieth century, the inspirational theories that emphasize the humanity of Christ have tended to prevail. This does not mean that the other views have been abandoned. It only means that modern man feels that his religion must involve him in the affairs of men. Christ stirs man to new concerns for his neighbors. (*S/R*, 22.)

Why follow Christ? (*S/R*, 23.) Finally, this question must be answered by each person for himself. If Christ was *only* a man, then we have an example, a prophet, a teacher, but no more revelation of God than we might expect to find in any unusual, superior man of virtue. We have no more reason to follow him than for following any other great man.

If Christ was *only* God, then man is left without an example, for Christ would then be divinity in disguise. He would not be able to really understand man in his condition.

If Christ was a God-man, we can say that God revealed himself in Christ. We have in Christ a clue to the nature of God himself—self-giving love. This love is bestowed on the just and the unjust, while we are yet sinners. God revealed himself as a man, suffered at the hands of those who sneered and jeered, died on a cross, and was resurrected that man might have insight into the nature of all creation—self-giving love.

■ Let each member of the class read silently *S/R,* 22 and then respond in turn to this question: On the basis of your understanding of Christ, how would you describe the contemporary mission of the church?

■ Select one of the affirmations of faith in *The Methodist Hymnal,* numbers 738-41, to read as a benediction.

■ Let the leadership team be prepared to give assignments for the next chapter of study and the members of the group be prepared to accept the assignments.

NOTES ON CHAPTER 3

Page 51: Bruce Barton, *The Man Nobody Knows* (Bobbs-Merrill Company, 1925), page 76. Copyright 1925 by the Bobbs-Merrill Company, Inc., renewed 1952 by Bruce Barton. Used by permission.

Read these selections in your Bible:
Matthew 18:15-20
The true church.

Acts 5:17-32
Obedience to God.

Romans 13:1-10
Accepting authorities.

4

□□

A PINCH OF INCENSE

The relation of the church to the state has been a persistent problem in Christianity. Should the state control the church? Should the church control the state? Should the state adopt Christian values and exclude all values of other religions? Should the state approve prayers to be read in school? Should the state pay preachers in uniform (chaplains) in the armed forces or veterans' hospitals? Has a Buddhist or Hindu ever been asked to lead in prayer at the opening of the U. S. Senate? Why is it unlikely that a professed atheist could be elected to the presidency (or any major office) of the United States? Should the state and church be separate? Can a person as a Christian be withdrawn from politics?

Many Christians today are genuinely disturbed by the exemption from taxes which the churches enjoy. Increasing numbers of religious groups are voluntarily paying taxes.

■ *As you arrive at your place of meeting, check the assignment chart for specific preparation to be made before the session begins.*
■ *Set goals for your study of this chapter as suggested on page 15.*

Taxation of business enterprises operated by churches poses a related problem. Churches are engaged in real estate, sports, oil, hotels, gambling, distilleries, and many other businesses, reaping tax-free profits.

What about public money for parochial schools? Is public bus transportation for parochial school children primarily aid to the child? Do the court rulings excluding prayer and Bible readings in public schools eliminate all religious instruction? (S/R, 24.)

■ To help members of the group gain perspective for considering the issue of church and state, look first at the general topic of Christ and culture. Have four perosns conduct a symposium. (Participants present prepared remarks. They need not interact with one another.) Use S/R, 25, parts A-E, Romans 13, and 1 Peter 2: 13-17. Let the entire group discuss this question: What are the implications of ideas presented in the readings and the Scripture for the issues raised in the introductory paragraphs above?
■ Divide the class into groups of four or five persons. Let each small group discuss one or more of the questions at the beginning of this chapter in terms of this question: What is the issue here between religion and the state? After ten minutes of discussion, let each group report. As they report, someone should summarize each principle and write it on newsprint or chalkboard.

SHOULD THE STATE CONTROL?

Much of the church history reflects Acts 5:29, "We must obey God rather than men." Peter would not obey the command of the secular authorities to stop preaching in the name of Jesus. His answer has been inspirational for hundreds of Christian revolutionaries, who have said the government had no right to control convictions. (S/R, 26.)

This problem of state control is an old one in the history of Christianity. It can hardly be denied that Rome put Christ to death at least in part because his preaching seemed to threaten the "peace." He was a disturber. One of his disciples was a political Zealot committed to the overthrow of foreign rule by violence! Actually, the Roman government was relatively tolerant of new religions, so long as they did not undercut the unity of the empire which the divinity of the emperor symbolized. To escape persecution Christians had only to show their ultimate loyalty and patriotism by putting a pinch of incense on the emperor's altar or otherwise acknowledging him as divine. Only in the last fifty years of persecutions, from Decius to Diocletian, did the government attempt to exterminate the Christians.

Constantine's Edict of Toleration in 313 which stopped the persecutions has been hailed as a great Christian triumph. Actually it was something less than that. Constantine legalized and subsidized Christianity, but he also sought to manipulate the church for the sake of political unity in the empire. He called the first great ecumenical council of Nicaea in 325, not to further religion but to stop the disrupting influences of the religious quarrels that had started.

Charlemagne was crowned by the pope in the year 800 on Christmas Day while he knelt at the altar. But Charlemagne, who governed Europe from the Pyrenees to the Danube, considered himself superior to the papacy and had actually gone to Rome to sit in judgment on the pope. On his own, Charlemagne called synods, promulgated religious laws, and supervised religion. He controlled the church.

Emperor Henry III in 1048 deposed the three men claiming to be the pope and appointed a new one. He enforced his decision with an invading army, condemning the three claimants, Silvester, Gregory, and Benedict, to "perpetual anathema." The new pope, the clergy, and the Romans granted the emperor the right to create popes and bishops. They promised that no bishop would in the future be consecrated until after the king had invested them in office. This situation did not change until the College of Cardinals was created in 1059. Election of the pope by the College helped prevent direct interference by the state.

This control of the papacy by the state was not unlike the control exerted by Napoleon, who sought the blessing of the pope to strengthen his claims to the throne of France.

In 1797 Napoleon invaded Rome and forced Pius VI into exile. The succeeding Pope Pius VII in 1801 entered into an agreement with Napoleon which reduced the papacy to a pawn in Napoleon's bid for empire. In 1809 when the pope tried non-co-operation, Napoleon invaded the papal states and imprisoned the pontiff. Even though a prisoner, Pope Pius VII refused to be Napoleon's lackey. This won him so many friends that when Napoleon was finally defeated, Pius VII emerged from prison as one of the strongest influences in Europe.

IN ENGLAND

Henry VIII not only controlled ecclesiastical affairs in England but had himself named "Supreme Head of the Church." His father was the first of the Tudor family of English kings. He arranged for his oldest son, Arthur (the older brother of Henry), to marry Catharine of Aragon, daughter of King Ferdinand and Queen Isabella of Spain (who had helped Columbus). When Arthur died, the pope gave permission for Henry to marry his brother's widow. When Henry became king in 1509, he said the pope was supreme.

Five of the six children born to Henry and Catharine died, and Henry began to believe that God had placed him under judgment for marrying his brother's widow. Mary was the only survivor, but no woman had ever ruled England.

When Henry sought to have his marriage dissolved, the pope refused. The pope was afraid the powerful monarchs of Spain would be angry with the church if he allowed the separation. Henry appealed his case to several universities. Their favorable responses encouraged him to act. Boldly he resurrected an old law which made appeals to Rome treasonable. He used this statute to intimidate the clergy of England. In 1532 they acknowledged him the supreme lord of the church. He made Thomas Cranmer, his advisor, the Archbishop of Canterbury. Cranmer then declared Henry's marriage to Catharine null and void. In 1534 denial of Henry's supremacy over the church became a capital crime—treason!

■ The "Chart of Key Questions" (Resource Packet, item 4) may be used here to help persons become aware of the relationship in time of powerful rulers to the crisis events in church history. See the Leaders' Guide in the packet for specific directions.

■ *Think silently:* If you lived in a Moslem country, how would you feel if you were required to accept Moslem religious practices?

Now, as one person reads aloud *S/R,* 26, other members of the group may follow the reading, underlining words or phrases that bear relation to the kind of situation described in the above question. (Pencils should be provided.)

Then, let the total group discuss these questions: Do you agree that modern Christians are now trying to force all Americans, whether Christians or not, to follow Christian customs? How is this coercion similar to or different from the Roman law that all people had to practice emperor worship? What rights does a non-Christian have in our nation?

Can you cite evidences that a similar kind of coercion is sometimes practiced within the church in relation to conformity or belief? What bearing does this attitude have on enforcing public piety?

In 1558 Elizabeth I became the ruler of England. She resolved to follow a middle road between Catholicism and Protestantism, with herself as the supreme governor of the church.

After Elizabeth, from James I in 1603 to William and Mary in 1689, the rulers of England sought to dominate religion. James I ordered all Jesuits to leave England. He required an oath of remaining Catholics. Catholics could not be guardians, trustees, lawyers, or doctors. Protestant dissenters who objected to Anglican bishops lost their pulpits. At great personal risk they established Separatist congregations. In 1620 the *Mayflower* carried the vanguard of thousands of Pilgrim and Puritan dissenters to America.

During the revolutionary times of Oliver Cromwell, Protector from 1653 to 1658, parliament outlawed the Church of England for a period of fifteen years. Under Cromwell a special commission managed religious affairs, examined candidates for the ministry, reduced marriage to a civil rite, destroyed ornate church altars, forbade Christmas festivals, and prohibited dancing.

When Charles II (1660-85) became king, Anglicanism was again established, much to the disgust of many Puritans. More than two thousand Puritan clergymen left their pulpits. This was the time of John Bunyan who wrote *Grace Abounding to the Chief of Sinners* while in prison and later *Pilgrim's Progress.*

Whenever the state controls the church, religion tends to lose. Hitler's manipulating of the Protestants and Catholics during his totalitarian reign was a disgrace which the blood of six million Jewish concentration camp martyrs will not let the world forget.

■ How have secular rulers attempted to use the church for their purposes or to attain their desires? Listen as one person reads aloud the account of Micaiah's prophecy before the king of Israel, 1 Kings 22:1-28.

Now divide the class into three work groups. If the class is large, more than one group may deal with the same issue. For ten minutes let each group consider the Scripture, search the material on pages 56-60, and record their findings according to the following assignments:

Group A will look for the various *purposes* for which rulers have attempted to force the church to support their desires.

Group B will look for the *ways* in which rulers have exerted their power.

Group C will try to determine the *effects* on (or the results for) the church from this kind of coercion.

Each group might consider the questions: Do parallel situations exist anywhere today? How do they affect the work of the church? Our writer says that when the state controls the church, religion tends to lose. Let each group decide, on the basis of their research, whether the statement is true or not. One person from each group should be prepared to report to the entire class.

CHURCH CONTROL OF STATE

The other side of the coin is the attempt of the church to control the state. Whether that control has been indirect, as with Protestantism in the United States, or whether it has been an open policy, as in Catholicism, the results have been disturbing.

The First Amendment to the United States Constitution denies Congress the power to establish a religion (meaning to give government support to it) or to make laws that curb the free exercise of religion. Many state constitutions guarantee freedom of religion and conscience and prohibit the use of public funds on behalf of churches. The founding fathers wanted to spare this country some of the dangers that had resulted from the direct support of religious institutions by the government.

We must not be misled, however, by the belief that there has been a "wall of separation of church and state." Protestant churches have dominated the history of this nation from its very beginning, and this is not to overlook the Roman Catholic contributions to our culture. Directly and indirectly, Protestantism made its influence felt in government and in the common ethos. The public schools when they emerged were in a sense Protestant schools, including in the curriculum, sometimes subtly, sometimes boldly, Protestant views.

Protestants, often unaware of their own manipulation of government, are shocked at the bold attempts of Roman Catholicism to manipulate. Reaction to Catholicism helped defeat Al Smith for president in 1928. That John F. Kennedy could be elected as the first Roman Catholic president in 1960 is a measure of our present acceptance of the religious beliefs of others. Yet it was necessary for Kennedy openly to repudiate the notion that his loyalty to Catholicism would displace his loyalty to his country. (S/R, 27.)

In Connecticut and Massachusetts, where Roman Catholicism is strong, laws opposing birth control and the spread of information about it reflect Roman Catholic beliefs. The courts have declared such laws unconstitutional. Now a controversy over abortion has arisen. In California and in twenty-two other states the controversy has become bitter. The numerous attempts of Roman Catholics to obtain public money for their parochial schools has caused widespread concern among non-Catholic and secular groups.

This concern has some foundation in fact. Roman Catholicism has for centuries claimed that it is above all states and has the divine right to direct every aspect of life. Vatican II's historic statement on religious liberty disappointed many people precisely because the statement claimed that Roman Catholicism is still the only true religion and that the demand for religious freedom "leaves untouched traditional Catholic doctrine on the moral duty of men and societies toward the true religion and toward the one Church of Christ." * (S/R, 28.)

Late in the nineteenth century the pronouncements of Pope Leo XIII clearly stated that the Roman Catholic acceptance of other religious groups was necessary until Catholicism should become the dominant religion. Then, of course, untrue faiths should not be given the same privileges as the true faith, as in Spain where Catholicism is favored. In Spain and some other countries, other religious groups cannot have easily recognized chapels, public funerals, or telephone numbers, nor do they have protection against fanatics who would destroy their property.

NOT A NEW STANCE

This is not a new stance for Roman Catholicism. From early in its history, the papacy has made historic claims of being a higher power than the state.

Rome insisted that the church there was founded by Peter to whom Christ gave the keys to the Kingdom. (Matthew 16:18 and following.) Since both Peter and Paul suffered martyrdom in Rome, it had a status higher than any other church. When churches like those at Alexandria, Caesarea, Antioch, and Ephesus quarreled, they found it convenient to appeal to Rome to settle various disputes, because the Mediterranean Sea separated Rome from involvement in their immediate hassles. Gradually Rome asserted its supremacy and declared that its primacy was passed from one bishop of Rome to the next through "apostolic succession." That is, the "power of the keys" given to Peter by Christ had been given to Peter's successors as head of the church at Rome.

Ignatius (pronounced *ig-NAY-shus*) about 115 strongly recommended the spiritual primacy of Rome. Irenaeus (pronounced *eye-re-NEE-us*) in 185 said all churches should agree with Rome "as a matter of necessity." In 190 Victor, the bishop of Rome, excommunicated all churches that did not accept the Roman date for Easter. The Council of Sardica in 343 gave any deposed bishop the right to appeal to Rome and said vacant bishoprics should not be filled without the decision of Rome.

After the bishop of Rome (the primary title of the pope even today) was acknowledged to be the head of the Catholic Church in Europe, the next step was to claim that the church is above the state. Late in the fifth century Pope Gelasius I said priestly power is superior to that of kings and emperors.

Pope Gregory VII in 1077 at Canossa, a small Italian town, made King Henry IV of Germany wait in the snow as a barefoot penitent to show the king that the pope was the higher power. In 1174 King Henry II of England went to Becket's tomb where he was beaten with three hundred strokes in order to have papal excommunication removed.

This power of the pope rested on the authority of the pope to stop the sacraments, without which one would be damned.

Not until the powerful pontificate of Innocent III (1198-1216), however, were the papal claims of power over the state fully realized. Innocent III controlled Europe from England to Constantinople. He mounted a crusade against the infidels outside and the heretics inside. When he became pope, he wrote letters to the rulers of Europe proclaiming himself God's representative on earth, less than God but more than man. He declared himself "Peter in the fullness of his power, appointed to judge all men, but to be judged by none." He made king after king surrender to him their kingdoms and receive them back as fiefs. Church totalitarianism reigned.

Pope Boniface VIII in 1302 made the same exalted claims, but the king of France as well as others opposed him. In the reversal of power that followed, France made the pope move to that country. The French dominated the papacy for seventy years. The popes were hardly more than French lackeys.

The inquisition which started in the thirteenth century was a diabolical form of church control. Regulations were established for the inquisition against heretics in 1229. Pope Gregory IX commissioned the Dominicans and Franciscans as inquisitors to exterminate the heretics. Torture was authorized in 1252 as a means of getting confessions. The inquisitor was the police, the prosecutor, and the judge. He was not subject to any law, only the papacy. Frequently the accused did not know of what he was accused or who were his accusers.

When a man by the name of Torquemada (pronounced *TOR-ke-MAH-da*) was chief inquisitor of Spain (1482-98), more than 10,000 people were burned and 100,000 imprisoned. A few years later, 1507-17, Ximénes (pronounced *ZIM-e-NEES*) burned 2,000 and jailed 40,000. As the state could not have traitors within its borders, so the church could not have heretics within its walls. A more fearful means of control could hardly be imagined.

AFTER THE REFORMATION

In 1542 Rome reactivated the Holy Office of the Inquisition to counteract the gains of the Protestants during the Reformation. It represented the Roman Catholic appeal to force and proved frightfully successful; thousands of evangelicals lost their lives.

Belligerent Protestantism also mounted drives to control the state. Calvin left a heritage of domination of the political sphere in order to display the glory of God. In Geneva between 1542 and 1546 Calvinists put fifty-eight people to death and banished seventy-nine. Calvin's Geneva punished adultery, nonattendance at church, dancing, striking one's parents, and criticism of Calvin's regime with heavy fines or even death.

The Thirty Years' War (1618-48) was the last great war fought mainly for religious reasons. The destruction in central Europe was abominable. Hardly a city in Germany escaped its ravages. Orphaned children roamed the woods like wild animals. Protestants and Catholics alike were using the state to achieve their ends, but neither could win decisively.

When peace came in 1648, those fighting had almost forgotten what they had been fighting for. But the war had one good result. People became disgusted with religious intolerance, whether Catholic or Protestant. Who has such certainty that he can take another's life?

Strict control of the community for the glory of God was carried across the ocean to America to become a part of our Puritan background. Those who differed from the Puritans in Massachusetts, such as Anne Hutchinson and Roger Williams, were driven out. The colony of Maryland was settled by English Catholics, but all Christians were welcome there. In time, the Catholics were persecuted.

A person should be expected to try to implement those things in which he believes strongly. One's religion is strange indeed if it has no bearing on everyday living. However, in the United States where Protestant intolerance has given way to the acceptance of many religious and nonreligious points of view, a new question has arisen: Whose convictions shall be implemented?

Roman Catholicism has claimed the right to assert itself as the only true religion. When officially recognized as such, it has not tolerated other faiths. When France acted to separate church and state in 1901 and 1905, the papacy sharply protested that its ancient rights were being violated. Pope Leo XIII (1878-1903) issued pronouncements denying liberty of conscience, speech, and teaching. He approved religious toleration only in situations in which Catholicism was not recognized legally as the *only* true religion.

Vatican II let loose a new spirit in Roman Catholicism, but the old views have not been officially repudiated. American Catholics, schooled in a democratic atmosphere, have not always fully agreed with the papacy. This disagreement may be seen in many instances of Catholic conduct in this country. Many American Catholics felt keen disappointment in the Vatican II pronouncement on religious liberty.

The problems of church and state are numerous and complex. And one must look at practice as well as official statement. Limitations of space prevent any detailed treatment of its many aspects. However, this much should be clear: Neither the church nor the state can bear the consequences of either one dominating the other. The implications of "separation" and "partnership" have not become clear. Separation implies that religion has nothing to do with politics, that religion is a private affair. (S/R, 29.)

THE PROBLEM REMAINS

So the problem of church and state remains. Every new court case seems to open up new principles: Should textbooks be supplied by the state to parochial school children? Are federal government loans to parochial and private schools for use in nonreligious enterprises really legal? Is released time for religious instruction legal? Can the Bible be studied as literature? If religious hymns cannot be allowed in public schools and secular songs can be, is the government thereby promoting nonreligion? Should income-producing property and businesses of churches be tax-exempt? Should laws regarding abortion be repealed? Should Amish children be forced to attend public schools? Many people do not want to go to war, so why should pacifists be exempted?

Final answers are yet to be found.

■ One or more persons may be prepared to summarize the history of the attempt of the church to control the state (pages 60-66). Simple charts of persons and events may be prepared on newsprint to aid in the presentation.

■ Go back now and read silently the first two paragraphs of "Should the State Control?" (Pages 56-57.) Consider the issue of Bible reading and prayers in public schools. Let one person read aloud, while others follow silently, S/R, 24. Study the wording carefully. Discuss: What limits or safeguards are set forth in the ruling? What opportunities do we have for action because of the Supreme Court ruling? How might some genuine education be started? (Read S/R, 26.) What new ideas come to you in the reading?

■ Have three persons read aloud the dramatic account of church domination of the state in the case of Anne Hutchinson (Resource Packet, item 3). The Leaders' Guide in the packet includes questions to be discussed after hearing the dialogue.

■ Discuss in the total group: In your mind is the issue of church/state relations one of all religious denominations and faiths united in their desire to maintain freedom from government control; or do you see the church/state issue as a struggle by Protestants, Roman Catholics, or persons of other faiths to manipulate the government? How can Protestants justify their own manipulation of government? Consider evidences of pressure exerted by the church on government: the blue laws, the Protestant chaplains in the House and Senate, government-paid military chaplains.

■ Let the leadership team be prepared to give assignments for the next chapter of study and the members of the group be prepared to accept the assignments.

NOTES ON CHAPTER 4

Page 62: *The Documents of Vatican II,* edited by W. M. Abbott (Guild Press, America Press, Association Press, and Herder and Herder, and copyrighted 1966 by The America Press), page 677. Used by permission.

Read these selections in your Bible:
Amos 5:18-24
The day of the Lord.
Matthew 25:31-46
The sheep and the goats.
Luke 10:25-37
The Good Samaritan.
Romans 8:31-39
More than victors.

5

□□

GOD WILLS IT—OR
DOES HE?

Whether the church shall be involved in the world is not a matter of choice. The question is how and to what extent.

The established churches with their large membership roles, country club atmosphere, and affluent appointments are very much involved. They are so much involved that the marks distinguishing them from private clubs or civic associations are sometimes difficult to find. So are the struggling rural churches which reflect their surroundings.

The same is true of those religious groups that try to withdraw from the world and cultivate the spirit. They depend on the very world they seek to disparage or avoid. Monks living in the deserts and mountains in the fourth century made baskets and other household goods so they could barter or sell them for bread.

Almost without exception the great monastic orders of the

■ *As you arrive at your place of meeting, check the assignment chart for specific preparation to be made before the session begins.*
■ *Set goals for your study of this chapter as suggested on page 15.*

Middle Ages, despite their vow of poverty, gradually became rich. The Cistercians (*sis-TER-shuns*) acquired gold plates and goblets and supplemented their plain food with fine wines. Despite vows of poverty, the Jesuits in the eighteenth century operated banks, colleges, and factories.

Churches are involved! Even if they do nothing, they are still doing something, for "doing nothing" supports the prevailing power. Churches are repeatedly accused of holding back, being conservative, in a period of great social upheaval. But they should not be accused of non-involvement. The *extent* to which the churches should be involved in such issues as the war in Vietnam, civil rights, open occupancy, water purification, air pollution, and so forth is an important question. But there is no question of involvement, for even silence displays that.

In the parable of the sheep and goats, Matthew 25:31-46, the goats are condemned because they did nothing. In astonishment they ask, "Lord, when did we see thee hungry or thirsty or a stranger or naked or sick or in prison, and did not minister to thee." (Matthew 25:44.) And Christ answers, "Truly, I say to you, as you did it not to one of the least of these, you did it not to me." (Matthew 25:45.) They were sentenced to eternal punishment. This inaction is what the prayer to pardon "sins of omission" refers to.

Being involved is not the question. How and to what extent should the churches be involved?

■ Jesus spoke of the responsibility of persons to be concerned for others. Listen as one person reads aloud Matthew 25:31-46. In a society geared to institutional charity or aid, how can this judgment of the nations be applied to the individual's attempt to obey Christ's teaching?

THE CRUSADES

The crusades were a strange phenomenon in the church. Pope Urban II initiated the crusades when he preached his famous sermon at Clermont, France, in 1095. Judged by results, it must be regarded as one of the most effective sermons of all times. The crusades began in 1096 and continued for nearly two centuries. Virtually all of Europe pooled their resources to recapture the Holy Land from the Turks.

Mohammed, the founder of the religion of Islam, died in 632. Before his death he instituted two rules which made expansion of the Arab states a necessity. He forbade the exposure of children, and he stopped tribal warfare. As a result the Arab population grew beyond the capacity of the land to support it. Damascus, Jerusalem, Antioch, Alexandria, Armenia, and Persia were overrun. The Moslems pushed across north Africa to the Strait of Gibraltar and then through Spain and into France. The Frankish leader Charles Martel stopped them at the battle of Tours in southern France in 732. But they held north Africa, Egypt, and most of the Near East for the next 350 years.

In 1071 the Seljuk Turks took Baghdad, most of Asia Minor, Antioch, and Jerusalem. They drastically curtailed Christian pilgrimages to the Holy Land. Fantastic stories circulated in Europe about the Turks' desecration of the holy places. That was the overt cause of the crusades; Christians felt that they must rescue the Holy Land from the infidels. (S/R, 30.)

On the other hand, practical, worldly causes were also present. Alexius I, ruler of Constantinople, appealed to Pope Urban II for help against the threat of the Turks. Urban responded, for the idea of a crusade presented an opportunity to unify Europe under the banner of the church against an outside enemy. Attention would be turned away from the internal troubles of the papacy. His own throne in Rome was in jeopardy.

Pope Gregory's program just twenty years earlier had left many bitter feelings. Pope Gregory VII had tried to purify the church by enforcing celibacy on the priests and by breaking the hold of the German rulers on the papacy. Enforced celibacy caused hundreds of married priests to resist. Riots and fighting occurred in the larger cities of Italy; many priests refused to leave their wives and children. Enforced celibacy represented a low view of marriage and a desire on the part of Gregory to keep priest's children from inheriting property. The struggle with the German rulers brought about the showdown between Gregory VII and Henry IV at Canossa in 1077. The pope humbled the emperor, but neither the pope nor the emperor kept his promises. The old rivalries smoldered.

Pope Urban II thought a crusade would unite Europe and would help him return to his throne which had been usurped. He thought a united Europe would improve the image of the church. He promised forgiveness of sins to all participants and eternal life to those who lost their lives. One chronicler said God invented the first crusade so the laity would have a new way to atone for their sins and win salvation. Participants could also win exemption from taxes, debts, and the like.

At Clermont, during Pope Urban's sermon, thousands drew their swords and began chanting, "God wills it, God wills it," which became the motto for all the crusaders. They committed themselves by sewing crosses on their garments or by burning them on their backs. (S/R, 31.) Peter the Hermit, a tall gangling man, carried a huge cross around Europe preaching the great endeavor. Literally thousands, without proper organization and provisions, started marching overland toward the Holy Land, slaying Jews along the way. In turn, brigands in the Hungarian forests and the Balkans butchered the crusaders. One group under Peter the Hermit reached Asia Minor, only to be slain by the Turks who piled seven thousand bodies in a huge pyramid as a warning to other invaders.

The crusaders inflamed Europe. Devout Christians, even women, wanted to rescue the tomb of Jesus from the infidels. Europe's leaders collected huge armies and launched the

71

first official crusade in August of 1096. It was church sponsored and church directed. By May of the following year the somewhat disarrayed armies conquered Nicaea, defeated the Turks, and made their way toward Jerusalem. Antioch fell in 1098 after a long siege. Jerusalem was captured and its inhabitants—men, women, and children—brutally slaughtered in 1099. The crusading leaders carved out kingdoms for themselves and dominated the area until 1144.

In 1212 the Children's Crusade, led by a shepherd boy twelve years old, proved disastrous. Thousands of children marched through France to the Mediterranean Sea which they expected to open up as the Red Sea did for Moses. Disappointed but determined, the children took boats from ports in Italy and France, but they never reached Palestine. Instead, unscrupulous traders sold them into slavery, thus writing one of the most horrifying chapters in the history of the church.

And so the crusades continued, without success, until the last of the European holdings in Palestine were lost in 1291.

Almost everything about the crusades was a denial of the gospel. Yet there has never been such an outpouring of religious fervor. Devout men, imbued with medieval piety, felt that no finer work could be done than the rescue of places hallowed by the life, passion, and resurrection of Christ. Trade increased, commerce flourished, universities began, knowledge widened, and the spirit of nationalism grew.

The church extended the crusades against heretics at home, thus creating the inquisition. (S/R, 32.) Churchmen agreed that Christians ought to fight as vigorously against heretics inside the church as against infidels outside. The extension of the crusades into an inquisition against other Christians marks a dreadful chapter in church history.

It is hard to see how the church could have been more involved in the world. Convictions drove the church to act as it did. The main conviction was that the church should dominate all of life. As the church had the power to implement its convictions, the crusades and the inquisitions were logical developments.

We who readily condemn the church's part in such endeavors should ask ourselves what we want the church to be. Do we want it to have political and economic power? Do we want it to have no such power? Do we think that the church should be wholly pure, without sin? Even Christ did not expect that. He told his disciples to leave the weeds with the wheat until the harvest (Matthew 13:24 and following), suggesting that the church in this world would never be pure. If we strip the church of power, can it still be *relevant* in the world?

Obviously, the matter of involvement in the world is not simple. Luther's warning should sincerely be applied. All of us are sinners, he said. All of us make mistakes. Therefore, when we think we are doing our very best, even when we pray, we should also repent and trust that God will somehow bring good out of evil.

A summary of church history would show repeated cycles: (1) stern faith that challenges the world; (2) relaxation of that vigor; (3) formalism; and (4) establishment of ties to the corrupt culture in which it is involved. (*S/R*, 33.) The cycle then begins anew with a recovery of stern faith. "Only a new withdrawal followed by a new aggression can then save the church and restore to it the salt with which to savor society." * Are we today in the last phase of such a cycle?

■ Ask class members to call out, without discussion, the ways they think the church has attempted to influence society during their lifetime. Have someone record these on newsprint or chalkboard.

Now consider the church's role in history around the year A.D. 1095. Have one person read aloud a portion of Pope Urban II's sermon which initiated the crusades (*S/R*, 31). Examine both the words of Pope Urban II and the above description of the crusades. What reasons were given for the crusades? Can you cite examples of similar reasons being given for the church's actions during your lifetime? How can such reasoning be justified?

■ Often the church consciously or unconsciously attempts to force submission to the church. Listen while five persons, prepared in advance, read one such account (*S/R,* 32.) How is submission to religious practice imposed upon society today? (See *S/R,* 26.) Why is so much importance given by the church to creeds, oaths, vows, and promises? Recall the religious phraseology in oaths, the Pledge of Allegiance, the Declaration of Independence. Why do people want this phraseology in oaths?

■ Use the "Chart of Key Questions" (Resource Packet, item 4) to help you examine your ideas of what you think the church should be. See the Leaders' Guide in the packet for detailed instructions.

■ Read again *S/R,* 33. What signs of the cycle of church history mentioned above do you see in the church today: (1) stern faith; (2) relaxation; (3) formalism; (4) ties to the contemporary world and culture? The question of whether we are now in the fourth stage is raised. Do you agree? Why? If we are in the fourth stage, what signs do you see pointing to a renewal of stern faith?

ST. FRANCIS

St. Francis (1182-1226) illustrates the tension of one who tried to be involved in the world and at the same time not to be part of it. As such he is a reflection of and a reaction to his times. Early in his life he revolted against the mercenary practices of his day, many of which his father, a moderately rich merchant, typified. In a war between the rich and poor in the town of Assisi in Italy, Francis put on armor and fought on the side of have-nots. He was captured and imprisoned for a year. Afterward he went to Rome and gave away all his money and clothing so that he could experience what it meant to be poor.

Returning to Assisi, he found he could not stand being a merchant. When Francis began distributing merchandise to the poor, his father hailed him into court. There in the court Francis stripped off his clothes and gave them to his father, signifying that he was beholden to him no longer. A priest took this act as a vow of renunciation and gave Francis a tattered robe.

For the first time in his life Francis felt liberated; he could live a carefree life. He begged for his food, repaired churches, and ministered to lepers in their colonies. Lepers were the first to call him a saint. Gradually a few men gathered about him. A new religious order formed around the cult of poverty which was a revolt against the commercialism of the day.

Francis knew that older monastic orders had begged and become rich or had worked and become wealthy. He resolved that he and those following him would never accept anything they could not use immediately and would work only to serve others. In poverty and in love, they would imitate Christ. (*S/R*, 34.)

Problems soon developed. Francis wanted no possessions, but he found himself and others making an idol of their poverty. He wanted his order to be free of rules, spontaneous in response to others, but as his followers grew he found discipline necessary. The keeping of rules led to the hypocrisy of legalism. In order to undercut idolatry and to foster service, he practiced self-denial, but his self-denial led to pride. In a time of learning, he rejected knowledge, for "knowledge puffeth up." He would not allow one brother to have a psalter saying he would become anxious about it, would have to have a bookcase, and so on.

St. Francis challenged the conscience of his time, but large groups of people could not live as he had lived. His begging involved him in the bourgeoise commercialism of his day. His objection to knowledge was unfortunate, for he did not realize that knowledge might have helped make his service of love more effective. Yet this helped preserve Christianity for the masses; the religious person is not necessarily the one who is learned and intelligent.

St. Francis represents both tension and strength in the church. He cultivated the cult of poverty while at the same time trying to accept God's creation and serve man.

■ The leadership team might look through current magazines for cartoons that depict the problems people face because of addiction to the desire for material possessions. They might display or circulate the cartoons. Contrast the attitudes displayed in the cartoons with the attitudes of St. Francis discussed in this chapter.

Discuss in the total group: What would be the style of life today for the person who feels the motivation felt by St. Francis? (See

S/R, 34.) How can those who do not take the religious vow of poverty—the shop foreman, the teacher, the salesman, the house-wife, the business executive, and the like—be obedient to Christ and still live a normal life? What are some of the challenges of being in the world but not of it? What problems are involved? What does it mean to you to be in the world but not of it?

THE CHURCH UNDER HITLER

Today we might ask ourselves if the church is becoming so secularly involved in the world that it is losing its identity. Is there a distinctive work that the church should be doing? Should the church be involved in marches for open occupancy and civil rights? The church in Germany during the time of Hitler may provide a clue about involvement. The church responded to Hitler in three different ways.

INVOLVED THROUGH CO-OPERATION

One part became so deeply enmeshed in co-operating with the Nazis that its message blended with that of Goebbels' propaganda office. These churchmen agreed with the Platform of the German Christians. The Platform was drawn up in 1932 and called for the formation of a church that would be truly German. The Platform called for a patriotic church, "rooted in the national character," "opposed to pacifism, internationalism, and Freemasonry," a church full of "fighters for freedom."

Some Christian ministers joined in that movement for a national church thinking they would be able to shape the development of Nazism from the inside. They could not condone nor condemn everything that Hitler was doing. Good seemed to be mixed with evil. Was Hitler to a certain extent good and right? He brought full employment to Germany during the depression, constructed super highways, strengthened old-age security, socialized hospitals and medicine, and made the trains run on time.

The majority of the church in Germany went along with Hitler's program. Many Christians found their own interests were being served by doing so. Others sincerely felt that by co-operating with the Nazis they would have the opportunity to witness to the good news in high places. Instead of directing the national church they found themselves rolled along by the Nazi machine, an indistinguishable part of it. They had bargained with a monster that demanded absolute loyalty and obedience.

In October of 1933, when the German bishops celebrated the 450th anniversary of the birth of Luther, they declared "We German Protestant Christians accept the saving of our nation by our Leader Adolf Hitler as a gift from God's hand." In the following year, after some churchmen had protested, these same bishops pledged "unlimited fealty to the Third Reich and its leader."

In the same year, 1933, Pope Pius XI concluded an agreement with Hitler bargaining thereby for special concessions to the Catholic Church, only to discover later that Hitler was using the church as a pawn. Pope Pius' pronouncement against Nazism as a way of life (1937) was too little, too late. It was too little because he did not break off relations and thereby throw the weight of the papacy against Hitler's program of doing away with the Jews. It was too late because the monster was already drunk with power. Pope Pius XII refused to denounce Hitler's treatment of the Jews in the hope that by maintaining relations with the Nazis he could aid refugees.

Rolf Hochhuth's *The Deputy* dramatizes this moral failure to speak out. (*S/R,* 35.) Other books show that *The Deputy* is based on historical fact and is not just an emotional outburst.

Lest we take pride in casting stones, we should note that the same criticism might be directed against the major church bodies in America on the question of racial segregation. The union of Methodism in 1939 was purchased at the price of a Central Jurisdiction—an ecclesiastical form of the fiction of "separate but equal." Even when national church bodies spoke clearly against segregation, local churches kept quiet on racial injustice. They did not want to disturb the peace or cause trouble. As one church leader said to this writer, "We don't have any race problem. The niggers stay in their part of town, and we stay in ours." The disturbed 1960's produced the inexorable and bitter fruit.

WITHDRAWAL

Another part of the church in Germany reacted to Nazism by withdrawing and attending only to those tasks that were "spiritual." They wanted to have nothing to do with political affairs. They attended to prayer, worship, the sacraments, weddings, funerals, and other traditional symbols of the church. No task is purely spiritual, however, and they could not escape awareness of political developments. Yet they withdrew as much as possible and made Christianity a private affair. In the face of overwhelming power such a witness is not without merit, but the transforming power of Christianity was thereby submerged, and that part of the church by its silence contributed to Nazism. Retreat from cultural problems is one of the dangers inherent in revivals of traditional ritual and sacramentalism.

RESISTANCE

A third part of the church in Germany protested Nazism— indirectly by reviving great Christian spokesmen of the past, directly by declaring their faith at Barmen and by attempting to thwart Hitler. Many of them had to flee from Germany; many went to prison; some died in concentration camps. In 1934 at Barmen, 140 delegates from evangelical Protestant churches in Germany issued a six-point confession opposing the identification of the Christian mission with national-racial policies. Karl Barth and Hans Asmussen were its authors. (S/R, 36.) It stands as one of the memorable confessions of our time. Dietrich Bonhoeffer returned to Germany from America, participated in a plot to kill Hitler, and after a long imprisonment was executed. Martin Niemoeller, a former submarine captain, went to prison for his Christian convictions. Such spokesmen served as a rallying point for Christian resistance, but they represented a comparatively small group in Germany.

After the war, in 1945, a group of Christians who had actually resisted Hitler's National Socialism nevertheless confessed before representatives of the World Council of Churches that they were also guilty: "We accuse ourselves that we didn't witness more courageously, pray more faithfully, believe more joyously, love more ardently." Another group of penitent German Christians helped build a modern cathedral on the ruins of England's 500-year-old Coventry Cathedral which the Germans bombed in 1940.

Who was involved? Who was responsible? Peter Weiss in his drama, *The Investigation*, lays bare far more than the horrible cruelties of the Nazi concentration camps. He points to the involvement and guilt of a whole nation, including even the Jews. One might say that he points to the involvement and guilt of Christendom, for Christendom had for centuries branded the Jews as killers of Christ, thereby generating untold prejudice and hate.

The Investigation shows Nazi leaders on trial for putting to death millions of men, women, and children for no other crime than being born Jews. They rationalized their actions saying they were obeying orders. Along with clerks, telegraph operators, townsmen, railroad dispatchers, and hundreds of other "little" people they said they were not guilty. They obeyed orders and stoutly defended their innocence in the name of duty and responsibility to their government. The reasons sounded very rational and reminded one of Pilate's hand-washing. But the cumulative evidence showed the involvement of an entire nation. (*S/R*, 37.)

The church witnesses even when it does nothing. The question is, To what does it witness? To its own stake in the status quo? To ideals that will benefit us but not others? To an identification of its gospel with national aspirations? To its own entanglement in worldliness? To brotherhood? To Christ?

The crusades show that we should examine our motives. St. Francis shows us that simple withdrawal into a cult of poverty loses the social impact of Christianity. The German church under Hitler shows us that compromise with a monster makes freedom of the gospel impossible. How the church in the past has become entangled is valuable to understand, but to say that the past is responsible for our present condition is to indulge in the fallacy that the *fathers* have eaten sour grapes and the *children's* teeth are set on edge. (See Jeremiah 31:29-30.)

Rather, let us learn from the past and prepare for our present tasks, knowing that all our actions are under the judgment of God, that they will be lighted and shaded by good and evil, and that none will last forever. Yet we must run these risks, trusting in God, lest we be numbered with the goats or judged like the man who buried his talent.

The question is not, Shall we be involved? We are involved. The question is, How can we in our culture be true to Christ, our Head?

■ Divide the class into groups of four to six persons. If the class is large, more than one group may deal with the same issue. Each group will study one of the three responses of the church to Hitler: (1) co-operated with Nazis hoping to influence the movement, but became an indistinguishable part of it; (2) withdrew and attended to only spiritual tasks; (3) protested Nazism by reviving Christian spokesmen from past, by declaring their faith, and by attempting to thwart Hitler.

Serious issues facing Christians today are war, poverty, and racial turmoil. How does the response of Christians today to these issues compare with the response of the church to Hitler? Let each group examine the three issues in the light of one of the three responses by the church to Hitler. What reactions today are similar to those of the German Christians? What reasons are given by Christians for responding in this way? What values are being upheld by this kind of response? What are some actions that are carried out as a part of this response? What are some results of the actions? When you compare these responses to the responses of German Christians to Nazism, which seems closest to God's will for us in these issues?

■ Two very opposite reactions of the German Christians are dramatically presented in S/R, 35 and 36. Let five persons (four characters and a narrator) be ready to read S/R, 35. The narrator should read all stage directions aloud as they are important to the incident. Then let seven persons (six voices and a narrator) read S/R, 36. The narrator will read the first two paragraphs. Then the six voices might read the next paragraph in unison. Each of the six voices will then read one of the truths.

Discuss: To what does the church witness even when it does nothing? Can you point to anything that would indicate that your church (you) has (have) witnessed to the faith—taken a stand against injustice and corruption?

■ Display the picture "Coventry Cathedral" (Resource Packet, item 8).

As you study the picture silently, ask yourself, "How can I in our culture be true to Christ?" Let this be the benediction.

■ Let the leadership team be prepared to give assignments for the next chapter of study and the members of the group be prepared to accept the assignments. See an assignment for three interviewers on page 93.

NOTES ON CHAPTER 5

Page 73: H. Richard Niebuhr, Wilhelm Pauck, Francis P. Miller, *The Church Against the World* (originally published by Willett, Clark and Company, copyright 1935 by Willett, Clark and Company), page 123. Used by permission of Harper and Row, Publishers, Inc., New York.

Read these selections in your Bible:
Matthew 16:13-23
"On this rock."

John 7:12-24
The source of authority.

Romans 12:1-13
Living in the body of Christ.

1 Corinthians 1:17-25
The foolishness of God.

6
□□□

BY WHAT AUTHORITY?

On every hand today authority is lacking. Everything is being questioned. Nothing escapes. Who knows what standard to use, what to believe, what to do? The old standards to which men once appealed have had their validity shaken.

When one reads modern literature, he is often aware that no universally accepted standards of authority exist. "Anything goes" so long as one can get away with it.

The present generation has become disillusioned. (*S/R*, 38.) Ism after ism, each claiming to be the final answer, has proved to be pseudo. The passing parade of idols has left in man a void. Man has learned to live for himself, the only thing of which he can be sure, but the high incidence of mental illness renders even that certainty a myth.

Jesus spoke of God as his authority, but many people do

■ *As you arrive at your place of meeting, check the assignment chart for specific preparation to be made before the session begins.*

■ *Set goals for your study of this chapter as suggested on page 15.*

not acknowledge any ultimate Being. Those who do acknowledge God fail to agree on just how God's authority comes down to man. Even one who accepts the Bible as authoritative does not escape the problem. He has to decide what portions of the Bible he will accept as more authoritative than others. Before he can decide this he must have a standard by which to decide. That standard will vary from person to person. Many Methodists can honestly say that the fifth article of religion is not too meaningful:

> The Holy Scriptures contain all things necessary to salvation; so that whatsoever is not read therein, nor may be proved thereby, is not to be required of any man that it should be believed as an article of faith, or be thought requisite or necessary to salvation.*

In this chapter we cannot trace all the ramifications of authority, but we can look at some biblical aspects of it at the beginning of Protestantism. In Chapter 8 the problem will again be considered.

■ You have reached mid-point in this unit. Evaluation of how the group is operating would help the leadership team as they plan for the remainder of this study. Before this session begins, select two persons who will act as observers during the session. They might watch for: evidence that leadership is shared by the group; signs of openness and trust, or the lack of it; domination of the group by just a few persons; withdrawal of persons and reasons for it; evidence of preparation; points at which insights came. Allow time at the close of the session for a report of their observations.

■ Let the leadership team, or persons assigned in advance, have prepared a bulletin board display of clippings, headlines, and pictures that illustrate the idea that traditional standards of authority no longer exist. Read silently S/R, 38. Can you cite instances that contradict the theme of the bulletin board or the selected reading?

INFALLIBILITY

On April 28, 1967, Pope Paul VI announced that the Roman Catholic doctrine of papal infallibility (that is, the belief that the pope cannot be wrong when he speaks on an issue of faith and morals) was the "most serious obstacle" to unity with other Christians. He further said that papal infallibility was a doctrine going back to the very formation of the church. It "sprang from the role Christ assigned us in the church, and which our tradition has sanctioned with so much authority." (S/R, 39.) Papal infallibility was not defined as a dogma until Vatican Council I in 1870, but the Roman Church for nineteen centuries has acted as though it could not be in error. "No salvation outside the church" was an early slogan.

Pope Innocent III (1198-1216) realized the greatest power that the papacy has ever known. From England to Constantinople, from Scandinavia to Spain, kings and princes bowed to him as if they were his vassals. He asserted the supremacy of the papacy over all other authorities. His power was not merely theoretical; it was actual. He declared that he was appointed to judge all men, but to be judged by none. He was the apostolic successor of the apostle Peter, vicar of God on earth, and his word was binding.

Thomas Aquinas (1225-74), the greatest Catholic theologian and teacher of the Middle Ages, discussed the authority of the church. Faith and reason, he said, are ways to the same truth. They do not contradict each other because truth cannot contradict truth. Aquinas (pronounced ah-KWY-nas) explores the reaches of reason, giving it a place alongside faith in solving the moral problems of man. Finally, however, the grace of the sacraments dispensed by the church is necessary for the full realization of the powers of reason. The church stands at the pinnacle of both faith and reason!

In the system of Aquinas, authority moves from the top down. The church is superior to all institutions. In Pope Innocent and Aquinas, infallibility received concrete expression long before Vatican I in 1870.

Ordinary men could see that the popes were not always

persons with high character. Too many men had despoiled the office with their worldly ambitions and immoralities. During what is called the Babylonian Captivity when the papacy was deeply involved in French politics and during the Great Schism when two and then three men claimed to be the true pope, people questioned papal authority. The mysticism of Meister Eckhart, John Tauler, and the Brethren of the Common Life in effect bypassed the position of the church as a mediator between man and God. The mystical way to God denied the infallible authority of the church.

In England, John Wyclif (1320?-84) also defied papal authority. Wyclif (pronounced *WICK-liff*) rejected the mass and appealed to Scripture as a basis for radical reform of the church. The Scriptures, he maintained, are superior to the papacy. He translated the Scriptures so every man could have the authority of the Word.

Because the Bible was the basis of his views on stewardship, Wyclif and his friends produced a translation of it in English. Rome had not yet permitted the laity the privilege of reading the Bible in their own language, although important people could do so. Wyclif's followers carried his ideas to the people and suffered severe persecution. The Council of Constance (1414-18) condemned Wyclif's teachings. This council ordered his bones to be dug up and burned—if they could be distinguished from other bones buried nearby. John Hus spread Wyclif's ideas in what is today Czechoslovakia and was burned alive by order of the Council of Constance.

■ The "Chart of Key Questions" (Resource Packet, item 4) will help you discover some of the key persons and issues related to the place of authority in church history. Consult the Leaders' Guide in the packet for specific instructions.

THE REFORMATION

Martin Luther's struggle with authority was also his struggle with infallibility. The claim of absolute authority was already centuries old in the Roman Catholic Church, but infallibility was not a required belief, nor was it required to believe that the pope controlled purgatory. Luther's struggle to believe brought the matter to a head. The immediate cause of his trouble was the selling of indulgences.

Indulgence papers had been common for many years. The popes had used them to induce people to go on the crusades, which officially began against the Moslems in 1096. Pope Urban II promised forgiveness of sins to participants in the crusades and entrance into paradise for those who lost their lives. Pope Innocent III made similar promises to get people to rescue Jerusalem from the Mohammedans, adding that a person could contribute money or outfit a substitute to go in his place.

The church could issue indulgences, because some people had more good works than they needed to get to heaven. According to this theory, the extra merits of Christ and the saints are in a bank on which the church can draw to help people who do not have enough merits. In exchange for money or other goods, the church then issued indulgences both for future and past sins. The church acted as a kind of exchange bank.

Pope Sixtus IV in 1476 granted absolution for the dead in purgatory to anyone who could pay the price. This proved to be such a good way to raise money that popes continued the practice.

By the time of the Reformation, indulgences accounted for about half of all the papal revenues. The traffic in indulgences was big business. Bankers often made loans and accepted the promise of an indulgence sale as collateral.

Obviously, the church in selling such indulgences was assuming the right to bind and to loose not only on earth but also in heaven. (See Matthew 16:19.) Sin was something a person could wash away by buying a piece of paper. Certainty carries a strong appeal for man, and the certainty of having present and future sins wiped out was comforting. (S/R, 40.)

But not to Martin Luther. He wanted to know the grounds on which the head of the church claimed such power. Papal control over purgatory was not required as an article of belief for Roman Catholics until Pope Leo X issued the pronouncement in 1519. In the following year Leo excommunicated Luther as a "wild boar" who was uprooting the Lord's vineyard. However, Luther had already accepted a new authority—the Bible interpreted by right reason.

When Luther became a monk and joined the Augustinian monastery at Erfurt in 1505, he intended to do enough good works to get passage to paradise. He tried the ways then current. (1) He performed prayers, religious pilgrimages, fasts, and works of asceticism, which meant punishing the body so as to uplift the soul. He practically starved himself, slept without covers on an iron cot in the cold of winter, said Ave Marias and Pater Nosters, appealed to the saints and apostles, and stayed awake at night to repeat extra psalms and invocations. Yet he never felt that he had done enough. (2) The second way he tried was the way of the sacraments, but this required confession of every sin that was to be forgiven, and Luther could never be sure that he had mentioned all his trespasses. (3) He would have tried mysticism, but he could not even begin; he felt he was too sinful to approach God, much less be joined with him in a beatific union. Luther exceeded all the requirements, but he felt he could not please God. Deep within his own heart he was afraid that he hated God and so could never keep the first commandment.

Luther continued until his illumination, which finally came through his reading of Scripture. He suddenly realized that God loves man in spite of sin. God's son died for us while we were yet sinners. We do not have to earn God's love. He freely gives it; we have only to accept. A Christian does good works not to *win* something from God but to *show* his joy and gratitude for what God has already done.

Luther called his discovery justification by faith. He felt released from feverish, self-centered attempts to save himself through his own works. God's love was his! He did not have to pretend he was earning it. His illumination showed him new meanings in Psalms, Romans, Galatians, and Hebrews; and he felt that the sale of indulgences was a mockery of the gospel. In protest on October 31, 1517, he posted the Ninety-five Theses, that is, ninety-five propositions he was willing to debate. (*S/R*, 41.)

Luther did not know at the time that Pope Leo X and Albert of Brandenburg (in Germany) had made a deal so that Albert could become the archbishop of Mainz. The pope and Albert had made the deal even though Albert was too young to be a bishop and was already holding two bishoprics, which was illegal. Albert could be named archbishop if he paid about a quarter of a million dollars to the church. Albert borrowed the money from bankers. The pope was to grant Albert the right to sell indulgences in his territory. Half the indulgence money was to go to the bankers until the loan was repaid and half to the pope, who was building the great church of St. Peter which stands today in the Vatican in Rome.

The reaction to Luther's ninety-five propositions was sensational. When challenged, Luther said Scripture has authority superior to that of popes and church councils. Despite debates, pleas, bribes, and threats Luther would not budge. In 1520 the pope branded him as a heretic. At Worms (rhymes with *forms*), a city in Germany, in 1521 he faced the might and pomp of Emperor Charles V and said, "Here I stand, I cannot do otherwise, so help me God!" Luther declared that he could not alter his convictions unless he was proved wrong by Scripture and right reason. By the latter he meant reason grounded in faith. In the depths of his being Luther knew that there could be no authority other than the living God who confronted him in Scripture.

But how was that God to be interpreted? Who could say exactly what God was saying in Scripture? Throughout his life Luther felt pangs of doubt; sometimes he felt despair, as if he were being overcome by the devil. Who was he to say that he was right and the church wrong? Did he have some private pipeline to God? He often became aware of his human frailty, his mistakes, but his conscience was captive in faith to God. Scripture in which he had found justification by faith was his authority. He trusted and lived and died in that faith, but he was never *absolutely* certain, for he was a man, not God. This was the heritage that he bequeathed to Protestantism.

The Catholic Church asserts an authority to which all believers must submit. By submitting and by doing what the church commands, the individual need not worry about salvation. He can rely on the church for salvation as one would rely on an expert plumber to repair the plumbing or on a skilled surgeon to remove an appendix. This promises a kind of certainty that eludes the Protestant.

The Council of Trent (1545-63) established twin authorities in Roman Catholicism—Scripture and tradition as interpreted by the pope. Tradition includes all the historic pronouncements and acts of the church, even Scripture. (*S/R,* 42.)

In 1870 Vatican Council I announced the dogma of papal infallibility: The pope cannot err when speaking officially on faith and morals. The pope, then, as the teaching voice of the church expresses authority in Roman Catholicism. He is the final arbiter.

■ To gain some knowledge of the climate that fostered the Reformation, review pages 85-89 of this chapter. Now, listen as one person (preferably a man) reads aloud and with force *S/R,* 40. Then let another person read with equal force, Luther's reaction to the existing conditions (*S/R,* 41). Luther believed that the only authority was God who revealed himself in the Scriptures. You might examine particular Scriptures to see how they influenced his Ninety-five Theses. The Letter of Paul to the Galatians is one example. Work in groups of four or five. Each group will search one chapter of Galatians for words or ideas that seem to be related to some statement of Luther in *S/R*, 41.

■ A panoramic view of church history is presented in "The Witnessing Church" (Resource Packet, item 5, record 1). As you listen to the record and look at the accompanying pictures in this book, look for evidences of ways authority has been exercised in, by, or on behalf of the church. Recall, if you can, from previous chapters in this book examples of authority being exercised in, by, or for the church. The Leaders' Guide in the packet includes discussion questions and detailed instructions.

THE CHURCH AND THE BIBLE

"Scripture interpreted by right reason" became the rallying point of authority for early Protestants. When the Bible was not clear, they turned to right reason—the reason of the man of faith, a reason inspired by the Holy Spirit just as the Scriptures were inspired by the Holy Spirit.

However, Protestants soon found that Scriptures do not speak to all seekers in the same way. Not only did quarrels occur between Catholics and Protestants but also between Protestants and other Protestants. Although Zwingli and Calvin both drew heavily on trends initiated by Luther, they were never able to come to full agreement with him. For many years Lutherans hated Calvinists even more than they did Roman Catholics.

We also have the spectacle of Protestants and Catholics vigorously persecuting radical groups in the Reformation known as Anabaptists. The Anabaptists took seriously the Sermon on the Mount which they tried to follow literally. Most of them rejected infant baptism, would not swear oaths, nor bear arms, nor hold public office.

It is very well to say we will take Scripture as our guide, but what Scripture? Are some books more important than others? How many books are in the Bible?

90

Protestants usually count thirty-nine books in the Old Testament. This coincides with the number established by the Jews of Palestine when they met at Jamnia about A.D. 100. However, the Jews of Egypt added the thirteen books of the Apocrypha to their Old Testament. The early Christians used the Greek version of the Old Testament, which included the thirteen extra books in it, because they understood Greek better than Hebrew and Aramaic.

Other questions also arise. Is the Bible infallible? Is every word equally important? Luther said church practices not specifically prohibited in Scripture were permissible. Thus, he could retain many rites and ceremonies and introduce new ones. Calvin regarded the Bible as a kind of code of law. John Knox of Scotland said aspects of worship not expressly commanded by God were idolatries.

Zwingli launched his reforms in Zurich (Switzerland) with the claim that he would keep nothing that was not in Scripture. He instituted a love feast in the place of the mass and removed ornaments such as tapestries, relics, crucifixes, frescoes, candles, and pictures from the churches. The Bible was his guide, but it was the Bible as he interpreted it. The Anabaptists broke away from Zwingli precisely because they could not find infant baptism in the Bible, a practice which Zwingli wanted to retain because of the ties between church and state in Zurich. He successfully defended infant baptism as scriptural and caused the death penalty to be passed against the Anabaptists for not complying.

On the Lord's Supper, Luther and Zwingli confronted each other at Marburg in 1529 and failed to agree. Luther stood by "this is my body," while Zwingli interpreted Jesus' words to mean "this signifies my body." Zwingli argued that Jesus did not literally mean he was a door or a vine when he said, "I am the door" and "I am the vine."

Heavy dependence on the literal words of Scripture caused many Protestants to keep women from teaching or preaching (see 1 Timothy 2:12), to insist that women wear hats in

91

church (see 1 Corinthians 11:4-15), and to forbid women having short hair. The Bible was used to justify slavery, and even today the Bible is sometimes used to "prove" that segregation is the will of God. On the basis of Exodus 22 witches have been put to death, and on the basis of Mark 16 Christians have handled poisonous snakes to demonstrate their true Christianity. On the strength of Deuteronomy 28 the poor have been condemned as sinners cursed by God.

Such biblicism also made for a certain rigidity which caused many Protestants (and Roman Catholics) to fight new truth, such as the theories of Copernicus and Darwin. That the earth revolves around the sun upset some notions about Joshua commanding the *sun* to stand still, and that man evolved into his present form over many centuries upset some notions about the creation account in Genesis. (*S/R*, 43.) Darwin's *On the Origin of Species* which appeared in 1859 seemed quite contrary to the six days of creation in Genesis. In 1925, the State of Tennessee passed a law (repealed 1967) that evolution could not be taught in the public schools, precipitating the famous Scopes trial.

Simple biblical authority is not simple at all. Embarrassment, contradictions, confusion, and contentions resulting from appeals to conflicting portions of the Bible have fostered doubts about the Bible as an authority and have caused people to seek other standards. Sometimes, of course, people are not even aware of how much their prejudices, biases, and reason are being used in their "biblical" authority.

■ Protestants usually cite the Bible as one important authority for them. However, the extent to which the Bible is authoritative differs from person to person.

Provide each person with a pencil and a sheet of paper. Let each one write his answers to these questions: When do you turn to the Bible for help in making decisions? What particular portions of the Bible do you seek and accept as authority? How do you decide? See *S/R*, 44. Does the Bible give answers for every kind of question —for example, those related to medicine or science?

If, in the previous session, three persons were each given the assignment of asking these same questions of two persons who are

not members of your church, let them report the answers they
received. Share your answers to the questions and compare with
those reported by the interviewers. What general conclusions can
you draw about the Bible as authority?

REASON AND SPIRIT

Luther appealed to "right reason" or "conscience," but he
believed that reason must first be enlightened by faith. Reason without the guidance of the Holy Spirit was for Luther
something to be shunned, especially in religion, for there
are things in religion that reason simply cannot fathom. They
are revealed. Reason could never discover them—such things
as the Trinity, how God could be in Christ, the Resurrection,
how to attain eternal life, faith, and so forth. Reliance on
reason tends to glorify man. Consequently, Luther had harsh
things to say about predecessors like Aquinas and Aristotle
who built systems of thought on reason. Calvin also distrusted
reason unless it is guided by the Spirit. Without the Spirit
the Bible presents man with a maze of dead texts. But who
can say whether the Spirit is guiding reason?

Still another group at the time of the Reformation believed in the immediate inspiration of the Holy Spirit.
Thomas Müntzer and other fanatics urged the destruction
of images and relics in the churches and created general dis-
order in Wittenberg in Germany. They claimed a direct
revelation from God was their authority. Luther maintained
that private inspiration could not contradict the written
word of the Bible, because the Bible was inspired and the
Holy Spirit would not contradict himself.

However sincere such inspiration might appear to be, it
always runs the danger of being a projection of one's own
whims and desires. Luther wanted all such claims of inspiration checked against the written word.

Unfortunately, a final, unquestionable authority is not
possible for man. He can rely on the Bible, use his reason,
and believe that the Holy Spirit is speaking directly to him,

and all three may have valuable aids for his living, but he dare not deify any one or even all of them. In deifying these, he simply deifies his own understanding of them and falls into the idolatry of other gods which the first commandment condemns. On the basis of a "true" interpretation of Scripture, Zwinglians, Lutherans, Calvinists, and Catholics put heretics to death.

Dispute over interpretation of the Bible has been a prominent characteristic of American church life for almost a hundred years. The American consensus—including a large part of the Wesleyan tradition—is that the best understanding of the Bible falls somewhere between (1) the view of the fundamentalist that if the Bible is not infallible (every part equally inspired) it is worthless, and (2) the view of the rationalist that it is no different from any other book (none of it inspired). Our views of inspiration and authority are not those we can express to one another in words; rather, our views are shown in the seriousness by which we attempt to live according to the mind of Christ. The life I live shows what I *really* think about the Bible, its inspiration and authority.

Is the Bible still a meaningful authority? (S/R, 44.) Yes, but one must not use it without his reason, for reason is also a gift of God. Without the restraint of reason, one might easily interpret the Bible to mean anything he chooses. Without biblical revelation to enlighten reason, one might easily come to believe in nothing.

■ Discuss in the total group: Where does the average layman come face to face with the authority of the church? What authority do the pronouncements of the General Conference or the annual conference or the stands taken by the official board, or the pastor, or the commission on education hold for the average church member? To what extent does/can the Council of Bishops speak for the church?

■ Hear the report of the team of observers. What changes should be made as a result of their observations? How will you begin to bring about those changes?

■ Close this session by reading aloud Matthew 16:13-23.

■ Let the leadership team be prepared to give assignments for the next chapter of study and the members of the group be prepared to accept the assignments.

■ At this point it is time to place your order for the fourth unit of study, *Faith in Search of Understanding:* Christian Theology as Witness to the Good News.

NOTES ON CHAPTER 6

Page 83: *Doctrines and Disciplines of The Methodist Church,* paragraph 65.

The foundation of the church is Christ crucified and risen.

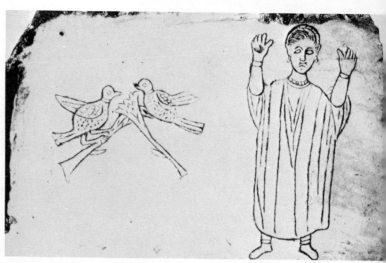

A drawing from an early Roman catacomb or underground burial place. The catacombs were used by the early Christians as places of refuge from persecution.

...rsecution unified the infant church.

3

4

...uins of a fallen empire, the Colosseum, where Rome martyred thousands of Christians.

5 Jerome (c. 347-419?) translated the Hebrew and Greek scriptures into Latin.

6 Augustine (354-430) was the most important Christian theologian four centuries after Paul.

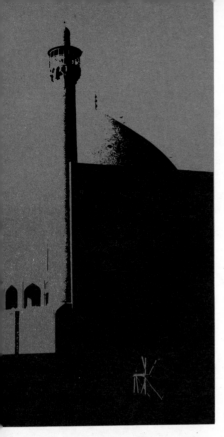

7

After the death of Mohammed (570?-632) Christianity suffered one defeat after another until Islam was dominant from Spain to India. The mosque and minaret shown here are typical of Islam.

8

Santa Sophia, once a Christian church and later an Islamic mosque, is a symbol of the defeat the church suffered at the hands of the Arabs. This building was one of the greatest achievements of the Eastern church.

9 *In the sixth, seventh, and eighth centuries, Christianity moved beyond the Mediterranean world into northern Europe and the British Isles. Augustine, Boniface, and Columba were important missionaries.*

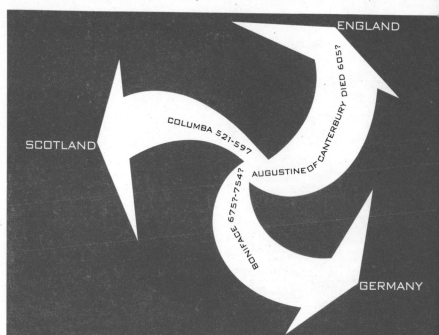

10 *Urban II (c. 1042-1099) was the pope who preached the sermon that launched the First Crusade.*

11

Francis of Assisi (c. 1182?-1226) was perhaps the greatest of the Christian saints in the Middle Ages.

2 *The corruption of the church in the late Middle Ages included selling indulgences. Christians then believed their time in purgatory could be decreased for a sum of money.*

13

John Huss (1369?-1415) was a Czech reformer who attacked the abuses of the clergy before Martin Luther. He was martyred. He is pictured here on trial.

14 *After he was excommunicated in 1521, Martin Luther was summoned befor the Diet of Worms. There he made his famous declaration of conscience refu ing to recant: "Unless I am convicted by Scripture and plain reason—I do ni accept the authority of popes and councils, for they have contradicted eac other—my conscience is captive to the Word of God."*

One result of the Counter Reformation was a revival in the Roman Catholic Church of a strong missionary surge spearheaded by the Jesuits and the Franciscans, who left their mark on the United States, as seen in this mission near San Antonio, Texas.

15

The Pilgrims were a group of English Separatists who fled England to this country to purify the church. In 1620 they founded Plymouth Colony, Massachusetts, in search of freedom to worship as they chose.

16

John Wesley (1703-91) preached often despite rioting and mob ridicule.

17

18

20

18. *Francis Asbury (1745-1816) was the man most responsible for the sound establishment of The Methodist Church on the American continent. He became bishop in 1784.*

20. *David Livingstone (1813-73) was a Scottish missionary and explorer who more than any other man opened Africa to the nineteenth-century missionary movement.*

Camp meetings were the center of wave after wave of religious revival on the American frontier in the nineteenth century. A Methodist camp meeting is pictured here.

Labor unrest, often violent, in the 1870's, 1880's, and 1890's, was one condition that helped give rise to the social gospel. Another was child labor. This and the two following pictures show railroad workers striking and children working as tenement-house tobacco-strippers.

22

24 *The General Conferences of The Methodist Church and The Evangelical United Brethren Church met simultaneously in 1966 and approved a plan of union.*

Read these selections in your Bible:
Jeremiah 31:31-34
The new covenant.

1 Corinthians 12:1-31
Parts of one body.

Ephesians 1:11–2:22
New life in Christ.

Ephesians 3:14-21
Prayer for unity.

Ephesians 4:1-32
One Lord, one faith.

7

□□□

WHY SO MANY CHURCHES?

Why do we have so many religious groups? In the United States alone more than 250 denominations! Many of them claim to be the only authentic voice of Christianity.

Some churches emphasize creeds or confessions as the essential thing; others have no stated creed or set of beliefs. Some emphasize liturgy, ethical rules, Holy Spirit baptism, the end of the world, and apostolic succession. Some believers drink poison or handle snakes. Some ban cosmetics. Some think Christians should withdraw from the world; some strive to control politics, economics and social affairs; some want to make way for the coming of Christ by subduing the ungodly with the sword. Is anything common and central in all the so-called Christian groups?

No creed has been devised which is broad enough to include all the Christian churches. The Apostles' and Nicene

---

■ *As you arrive at your place of meeting, check the assignment chart for specific preparation to be made before the session begins.*
■ *Set goals for your study of this chapter as suggested on page 15.*

Creeds have wide acceptance but in scores of churches they have no authority whatsoever.

Most Christian churches use the Bible in some form, but not all of them would agree on how it should be interpreted.

Some groups put great store by baptism, so that baptism might be considered a common practice. Even Roman Catholicism will accept the baptism of other churches. However, various forms of baptism are employed ranging from pouring, sprinkling, and immersing to no outward baptism at all.

Even though the Lord's Supper is widely celebrated in Christendom, the forms vary greatly. The Roman Catholic sacrifice at the altar bears little resemblance to the breaking of bread among Wesleyans.

Similar differences exist with regard to the ministry, liturgy, discipline, prayers, and almost anything else one cares to mention.

When the World Council of Churches was formed in 1948, it made acknowledgment of "our Lord Jesus Christ as God and Savior" the sole requirement for membership. For those who call themselves "Christians" this would seem to be a reasonable requirement, but again this automatically excludes some groups—the Unitarians and Jehovah's Witnesses, for example. Other groups exclude themselves saying the requirement is too loose, that belief in Christ as God and Savior can mean almost anything, and they choose not to be associated with such an organization.

But in spite of all our interpretations, Christ does in some sense remain the one common element in Christianity. Christians might not agree on his humanity or his divinity, on his Resurrection or his Atonement, on his Incarnation or his Second Coming, but Christ nevertheless remains central. We have no agreement of minds, but all Christians do acknowledge Christ. Beyond that, disunity looms.

Inside and outside the church embarrassing questions arise. What happened to one Lord, one faith, one baptism?

(*S/R,* 45.) Do so many voices indicate that Christianity has no truth? If it has, what is it? Is there any defense of the separation of the churches? (One crass observer has noted that all of them seem to take a collection.)

■ The leadership team might ask the church librarian or the local librarian to help them prepare a display of books dealing with the histories of the various denominations represented in your locality. Biographies of the founders or outstanding persons of the denominations might be included. Place 3x5 cards or a sheet of paper and a pencil with the display for those who wish to sign out a book to read. You might plan an additional session to hear reports by those who read some of the books.

DIVISIONS AND FREEDOM

In spite of the great number of denominations in Christianity today, there is not as much diversity as one might at first conclude from looking at a list of churches. Of the more than 250 denominations in the United States only a few of them have large memberships. Ninety per cent of the Christians in America can be found in about eighteen churches. This means that the remaining churches have very small memberships, often no more than a few thousand believers. If churches are grouped in denominational families, then ninety per cent of the Christians in America would be found in about a dozen such groupings. This is the reason why Protestants find so little difference in churches throughout the country. A few denominational families embrace the great majority of them, and these denominational families have a common heritage in the Reformation.

While denominations have greatly multiplied in the last century, we must not suppose that Christian disunity began with Protestantism in the sixteenth century. Acts 4:32 pictures the thousands of people who become Christians on the Day of Pentecost and shortly afterward as having "one heart and one soul," thereby implying unity in the earliest Christian community.

110

The exhortations to unity and love in the last seven chapters of the Gospel of John, however, clearly imply divisions within the early church. First Corinthians indicates divisions at Corinth. The entire letter points to quarrels and dissensions. In Chapter 1 Paul begs the people to have no divisions, for Christ was not divided. In Chapter 12 he asks that their unity be like that of the body whose many members are united even though they have different functions. "There are many parts, yet one body." In Chapter 13 Paul, using some of the most beautiful language in the Bible, depicts love as the way to unity. All of this indicates division within the early church.

Obviously, the early church had divisions; but the Roman Catholic Church dominated the Medieval Ages for more than a thousand years, leaving the impression that Christianity was one and that the great divisions in Christendom came with the Protestant Reformation. Actually, however, many divisions occurred within Catholicism in the Middle Ages. The Roman Catholic Church normally absorbed its dissenters in new religious orders which allowed many groups to develop with their own emphases while remaining in the mother church.

■ To understand that disunity did not begin with Protestantism in the sixteenth century but was prevalent among the early Christians, study the writings to the New Testament churches. Divide the class into study groups of six to eight persons. Each group may study one of the following scriptural passages: 1 Corinthians 1:10-17; 3:1-9; 2 Timothy 2:14-26.

Use these questions to guide your study of the Scripture: What were the causes of disunity discussed in this passage? What solutions are suggested? What similar situations exist in the twentieth-century church? What solutions are possible? A reporter from each group should be prepared to share the conclusions of his group with the entire class.

THE REFORMATION EXPERIENCE

The Protestant reformers of the sixteenth century were united in their rejection of Roman Catholicism and in their acceptance of the Bible as a primary source for religious truth. This was their over-all unity. But they did not all reject Roman Catholicism for the same reasons, nor did they find the same truths in the Bible. Economics and social factors in addition to the nature and means of salvation had a lot to do with the rejection of Roman Catholicism. When the Protestant reformers appealed to the Bible, they found that it could be read in many different ways, and early divisions among them resulted.

One of the great truths of the Reformation is that each man is finally responsible directly to God. For this reason men were expected to read the Bible and judge for themselves. This prompted the reformers to establish schools and to translate the Bible into the language of the people. Martin Luther called for public schools to train men for the church and the state as early as 1524, and in 1528 the first public school system since the days of ancient Rome was created in the German state of Saxony. Luther translated the New Testament into German in 1522 and published the entire Bible in German in 1534. His translation helped shape the future of the German language.

By appealing to the Bible and right reason, by disavowing papal authority, and by making each man responsible to God, the reformers broke through the ecclesiastical chains of a thousand years and established a principle of freedom that is central in Protestantism. This implies the freedom to establish a separate church if one wishes to do so.

The inherent principle of freedom did not come to the forefront in Lutheranism until the time of Philip Spener (pronounced *SPAY-ner*). While Spener himself did not separate from the Lutheran state church, other followers did—notably the Moravians.

This influence of the pietists carried over to John Wesley and Methodism where the principle of freedom again became manifest in a number of splinter groups. We have many denominations in Protestantism today; they testify to the basic freedom in the general Protestant position.

■ The principle of freedom is central to Protestantism. On the basis of the preceding material in this chapter, analyze the relationship of that principle to the experience of the Reformation and to the multiplicity of denominations existing today. Use the "Chart of Key Questions" (Resource Packet, item 4). Detailed directions are given in the Leaders' Guide in the packet.

TO AMERICA

Exiles who fled from England when Mary, an ardent Roman Catholic, became queen in 1553 found refuge with Calvin in Geneva and appropriated many of his beliefs and practices. When Elizabeth became queen in 1558, they returned to England and became the core of those who wanted to purify the Church of England of *all* popish elements. Consequently, they were called *Puritans.* Those who wanted to separate from the Church of England were called *Separatists.* Those who wanted a congregational form of organization rather than episcopal were called *Congregationalists.* Others were known as Presbyterians, Dissenters, and Independents.

The Puritans hated everything Roman Catholic. Puritan ministers would not wear vestments. They refused to use a ring in marriage ceremonies because it suggested a sacrament. For the same reason they often did not bury the dead with religious rites. They made the Bible their "sole" authority and enacted many of the rules commonly associated with the name *Puritan.*

Out of this same background came the Pilgrims and the Puritans who came to America. Hounded by English officials, they left England and went to Holland. On September 6, 1620, one hundred and one Pilgrim Fathers set sail in the *Mayflower* for America, with John Robinson's prophetic words ringing in their ears: Surely God did not reveal everything to Luther and Calvin; surely he has more light to break forth from his word.

113

George Fox, the English founder of the Quakers, insisted on religious freedom despite repeated imprisonments, fines, and maltreatment. Guided by the Spirit, he left his relatives in 1643 and began his wanderings. He would have no vestments, no commissioned ministry, no sacraments, no ritual, and no creed. He regarded the Bible highly but believed that the same Spirit that guided the prophets and apostles was also guiding and revealing truth to him through the Inner Light. Like the Puritans, he advocated a sober kind of life without amusements and luxuries.

WHY SO MANY GROUPS?

Does this background begin to suggest why there are so many groups within Christendom? No easy answer can be given but among the factors accounting for the number of groups are: (1) changing social conditions; (2) different understandings of religious and biblical ideas, and (3) variations in human nature itself.

Religion is such a personal thing that those who take it seriously want fellowship with those who think similarly. Fellowship normally develops along certain class lines, and new groups form even though the New Testament leaves Christians with the overwhelming impression that they should be united in love and worship. (S/R, 46.)

A strong case can be made for social conditions as the source for our denominations. As churches grow large, they become entrenched in the cultural mores and find biblical ambiguities to support social evils such as war, slavery, inequality, and privilege. Upper classes may lose interest in the poor. These problems cause deprived groups to feel neglected and to break away in order to emphasize those practices and beliefs which will establish their identity. (S/R, 47.)

Doctrines undoubtedly are a factor in the formation of new religious groups, but social factors seem to be equally significant. The episcopal (bishops), presbyterian (elders) , and congregational forms of church government have been drawn from the New Testament, but they also fit neatly into the political experiences of the various groups that insist upon them. The large churches are in general characterized by broad social interests; members are born into them; they are allied and aligned with large territories; they emphasize the universalism of the gospel and adjust to the morality of the majority.

The small churches, or sects, are usually characterized by narrower ethical interests. They frequently withdraw from worldly society; their members join by voluntary choice; they are exclusive and individualistic in their appeals, and emphasize certain key doctrines as if they comprised the whole of Christianity. The small religious sects usually rise from the ranks of outcast minorities, the poor, and those who have insufficient representation in the larger, established churches.

THE ORIGIN OF METHODISM

Methodism with its many splinter groups illustrates how social conditions and religious convictions combine to produce new churches. Methodism was born because the Church of England had become complacent. England in the eighteenth century had two classes of people—the rich and poor. The Anglican church catered to the former, leaving the masses of the poor to their own devices.

John Wesley, through his reading of William Law, Jeremy Taylor, and Thomas à Kempis, became convinced that personal dedication and a strict ordering of one's total life were essential to religion.

Wesley's religion was singularly unsatisfying until his heart was strangely warmed at Aldersgate Street in 1738. There his earlier resolve received the motivation of a heart on fire with love and trust in God and his new ministry began.

Wesley never parted from the Church of England, but soon after his death his followers did. Methodists in America

115

under the necessity of frontier conditions formed themselves into a separate church at the Christmas Conference of Baltimore in 1784, just a few months after Wesley ordained Thomas Coke as "superintendent." The Christmas Conference appointed Thomas Coke and Francis Asbury as superintendents (bishops), and a band of tireless, untutored preachers began evangelizing a new world.

EARLY SPLITS AMONG METHODISTS

Social conditions in America soon dictated changes. A group of ministers led by James O'Kelley strenuously objected to the autocratic power and life tenure of bishops. In 1792 they initiated the first schism in American Methodism by forming the Republican Methodists. The episcopal system offended their democratic spirit. In 1830 quarrels over freedom of speech and lay representation in conferences brought about the establishment of the Methodist Protestant Church in which authority rested with the people rather than the clergy.

Although the Methodists opposed slavery and in the General Rules of 1784 demanded the gradual emancipation of slaves, the Negro question caused splits in the young church. Negroes felt the sting of racial segregation in white churches, and in 1816 formed the African Methodist Episcopal Church in Philadelphia and four years later the African Methodist Episcopal Zion Church in New York. In succeeding years several other Negro denominations were formed, and in 1845 the question of slavery separated the main Methodist body into Northern and Southern branches. The Methodist Episcopal Church, South, underwent a further separation in 1870 when the Colored Methodist Episcopal Church was established, withdrawing Negroes from the Southern churches.

In 1934, the Methodists adopted a Plan of Union which resulted in 1939 in the merger of three Methodist bodies into The Methodist Church. The merger compromised the question of racial equality by creating a Central Jurisdiction for Negroes, which has been phased out in the Methodist-E.U.B. union of 1968. (*S/R,* 48.)

Some Methodists believed liberalism was too influential in Methodism and protested the 1939 merger. Among these who did not merge and started new churches were the Bible Protestant Church, which emphasizes verbal inspiration of the Bible and premillennialism, and the Southern Methodist Church which advocates racial segregation.

In England a hundred years after Wesley, William Booth withdrew from the Methodists. He said their well-appointed London churches had no place for the men like those he was rescuing from the sewers of life. Methodists had become like the Anglicans of Wesley's day. Booth founded the Salvation Army to fill a need being overlooked by complacent congregations.

The Pentecostal movement is another illustration of how a group has arisen because of dissatisfaction with the emphases of the major denominations. (*S/R,* 49.)

■ If the filmstrip *The Story of John Wesley* is in your church library or available from your annual conference board of education, you might like to plan an additional session to show it.

HUMAN NATURE

So far we have discussed changing social conditions and different understandings of religious and biblical ideas as reasons why there are so many religious groups. What about the third possibility, that human nature itself has something to do with so many separate churches?

One aspect of the way human nature has contributed has already been suggested in the section above. Some persons start smaller churches because they do believe their views and feelings are not adequately appreciated in the larger

117

churches. When one has deep convictions that are not welcomed, or when one feels that other members discriminate against him because his economic position and social status are lower than theirs, he may leave the larger group and try to draw around him those who value him and his opinions. Small sects begin sometimes in just this way.

Another way in which human nature has led to the establishment of new groups is the need for security. What I mean is this. Some of us have a greater need than others *to be told* what to believe and how to act. In a matter as important as religion but which lacks scientific proof, in a world so threatened by destructive forces, in a society where upheavals and uncertainties may suddenly appear, where segregation by social and economic classes as well as races is widely practiced, many people will follow any leader who seems to be sure of what he believes and can offer some "proof." This "proof" may be one or more kinds: (1) tradition; (2) the Bible; (3) direction from the Holy Spirit.

1. "Tradition" is a means of certainty for Catholics. The church has developed its beliefs and organization over a period of twenty centuries. This continuity going back to the time of Peter is, according to Catholic doctrine, the greatest source of certainty.

2. The Bible is a source of certainty for most Protestants. The exact nature of that certainty is not a unanimous view, however. Since all non-Catholics do not agree, the difference in the way the Bible is interpreted has caused splits in the church. For instance, the Church of Christ insists that the church today is to follow the pattern of the primitive church and add nothing not found in the New Testament. For that reason, persons in that church have the Lord's Supper every Sunday, baptize by immersion, and do not use any kind of musical instrument in their churches. Some groups say they are loyal to the Bible when they handle serpents. Beneath all groups who wish to follow the Bible as literally as possible

is this quest for religious certainty—a quest closely related to a need of human nature.

3. The third group is that made up of people who believe they are directed by the Holy Spirit. They too seek certainty that they are living according to the will of God.

■ Have a symposium panel. (Several persons present prepared remarks. They need not interact with one another.) The panel should be made up of representatives—a minister, a priest, or an informed layman—from the various denominations or religious sects in your town or community. Each member of the panel should, in a brief period of time, state the main points in the doctrinal beliefs and religious practices of his church. Questions may then be addressed to the speakers by the members of the class. To what extent was each denomination or sect a result of changing social conditions, different understandings of theological ideas, or variations in human nature itself? Some questions should arise out of the preceding paragraphs in this book and S/R, 47 and 49. (This means that members of the symposium panel should have copies of the study book and the book of selected readings prior to this session.)

■ You might plan an interesting follow-up. Ask the members of the symposium panel to arrange with a small group from one of their adult classes to meet with a small group from your class so that you might share with them insights from this discussion. This could serve as a springboard for more attempts of "living-room dialogue" and, perhaps, some concerted efforts for community action. Any such groups should report their experiences to the entire class.

■ If the symposium panel is impossible, another approach to the same idea would be for class members, prepared in advance, to make short reports about the various denominations represented in your town or community. Standard encyclopedias or handbooks on denominations will provide the necessary information. These are available at most public libraries. The librarian or your minister might help you locate them.

TRAGEDY AND GLORY OF SEPARATION

Our separated churches are both a tragedy and a glory. They are a tragedy because they witness against the spirit of unity which pervades the New Testament, reaching a climax of fullness and beauty in Ephesians. Ephesians 1:10 declares that the mystery of God's will is to unite all things in Christ, things in heaven and things on earth.

119

Yet the body is not united. It is scattered and broken by divisions. Christ died that the wall of hostility dividing men might be broken down and that all might be reconciled "to God in one body through the cross." (Ephesians 2:14, 16.) The author of Ephesians prays that all may see the breadth and length and height and depth of the love of Christ. (Ephesians 3:14-21.) "There is one body and one Spirit, just as you were called to the one hope that belongs to your call, one Lord, one faith, one baptism, one God and Father of us all, who is above all and through all and in all." (Ephesians 4:4-6.) The writer pleads for attainment of maturity and unity of the faith in the fullness of Christ so that we may no longer like children be "tossed to and fro and carried about with every wind of doctrine." (Ephesians 4:13-14.) He exhorts us to put away falsehood and to speak truth, "for we are members one of another." (Ephesians 4:25.) Present Christian disunity must stand as a tragedy. (S/R, 50.)

On the other hand, the separate churches also have a glory. The various churches allow for the development of a diversity of gifts. They witness to the freedom that men have in Christ. But this freedom and diversity of gifts can be a glory only if toleration, co-operation, respect, and love toward others prevail. If this is the case, then we have unity in diversity rather than separation and divisiveness. Given the vast differences in human nature, personalities, and backgrounds, one might even suppose that such unity in diversity has advantages over organic union. Diversity of church forms allows individuals to develop and express their gifts. But such diversity can hardly build up the body of Christ if it is not permeated with love. (S/R, 51.)

Diversity does not necessarily mean separation. Men need not worship in the same manner, have identical practices, church organization, or beliefs. Diversity is an expression of freedom, a precious heritage. Diversity with love and co-operation symbolizes the parts of the body of Christ working together for the good of all. Diversity without love and co-operation with others symbolizes the brokenness of the body of Christ.

The key question is not whether we have a multiplicity of churches but whether that multiplicity of churches is unified in love so that the members of the body of Christ work harmoniously together for the common good.

■ Let one person read aloud S/R, 50. Another will read aloud S/R, 51. Members of the class should follow the readings silently.

Discuss in pairs: Can you cite illustrations to support the idea that cultural or theological reasons usually given for separate denominations may be just excuses to retain separateness? In what ways might the influence of the church in the world be weakened by a lack of unity among denominations? Does the emergence of sects necessarily mean that the historic churches have been unfaithful witnesses? Why? Why not? What kind of reformation is needed within the church? What signs of apathy do you detect in the church? Who is the church?

■ What progress is being made toward unity? One person may be prepared to share stories and pictures from current newspapers, secular magazines, and church periodicals related to moves toward unity. News of the recent EUB–Methodist union would be of particular interest.

■ You might close this session by singing together "In Christ There Is No East or West" (*The Methodist Hymnal*, 192) .

■ Let the leadership team be prepared to give assignments for the next chapter of study and the members of the class be prepared to accept assignments.

Read these selections in your Bible:
Genesis 11:1-9
The pretensions of man.

Psalms 8:1-9; 144:1-4
What is man?

John 18:33-38
What is truth?

1 Corinthians 2:1-16
The power of God.

8

□□

I BELIEVE—BUT WHY?

What is truth? This query troubles men today as much as it did Pilate when he asked Jesus the question. We can imagine Pilate sadly and with a tone of resignation putting the question to Jesus. Caiaphas had given Pilate one point of view; the man before him was saying that he had "come into the world to bear witness to the truth"; and the people were clamoring for the release of Barabbas and the death of Jesus. In the face of these conflicting claims Pilate raised his question, "What is truth?"

We might very readily say that Jesus answered the question saying, "I am the truth." But then we would need to say exactly what he meant, for certainly it is not apparent to the ordinary reader. Pilate had no answer to the question he asked. He had no basis on which to frame an answer. He might well have been a cynic or skeptic like many of us, uncertain and apprehensive. How do we resolve conflicting

---

■ *As you arrive at your place of meeting, check the assignment chart for specific preparation to be made before the session begins.*
■ *Set goals for your study of this chapter as suggested on page 15.*

claims? On what basis do we accept or reject something pertaining to religion as true?

I BELIEVE ONLY WHAT I SEE

Many of us are hardheaded and would say, "I believe only what I see." In this we would be spiritual brothers of doubting Thomas: "Unless I see in his hands the print of the nails, and place my finger in the mark of the nails, and place my hand in his side, I will not believe" (John 20:25). This obviously is an ancient basis on which men have made distinctions. Oriented as we are toward science and its methods, we probably use it even more today as a way of deciding what is true. But on this basis, we would hardly be able to believe in any of the acts of Napoleon, the events of the American Civil War, or in the existence of Tibet or any place that we had not seen. We might say we believe because other people have reported it to be so. But that only removes us further from the actual seeing, and we might well question the one who reports.

David Hume is sometimes called "the complete modern pagan." He used "I believe only what I see" as the basis for one of the most devastating attacks ever made on Christianity. He made the attack in his "Essay on Miracles" about the middle of the eighteenth century. In his essay he argued that sufficient testimony to justify believing in miracles is impossible. Our knowledge comes from experience, from what we can see. Our experience testifies to the uniformity and regularity of nature. We see that day and night follow one another ceaselessly. We see the tides come in and go out with a regularity that can be timed to the minute. We see men die, and we see them buried, but we do not see them come back from the grave. These are truths borne out by present and past experiences of actually seeing.

If we are to believe in a miracle, Hume said, we must discount this regularity of nature. Rather than do that, he

123

argued, we might consider if it is not far more likely that those who report miracles are lying or mistaken.

Hume also struck at the heart of science by showing that no one can prove any absolute connection between a cause and an effect. When one billiard ball hits another so that the second ball falls into the pocket, we cannot prove that the cue striking the first ball caused the second one to drop into the pocket. We assume that the one caused the other, said Hume, simply because we are accustomed to doing so. We assume the two go together. We cannot prove it just because we see it. (S/R, 52.)

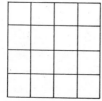 ■ To help you evaluate the idea "I believe only what I see," look at the drawing. How many squares do you see? Let several persons say how many squares they see in the drawing. Only those squares that each person can see exist *for him*. How can this fact be related to ideas presented in the preceding paragraphs?

I KNOW IT BECAUSE I FEEL IT

Some people cannot say why a particular belief is true; they just know it is true because they feel it so strongly. "I *know* that my Redeemer lives" (Job 19:25, italics mine) is often quoted with passionate feeling. Scholars tell us that the words in Job do not refer to Christ, but we quote and sing them to that effect anyway. This dependence on feeling is one of the historic marks of pietism and Methodism. It has definite limitations, but it also has the strength of great emotion.

Emotional fervor and deep inward feeling characterized the development of evangelical pietism. This religious attitude fed directly into Methodism. In the century after Luther, his followers tended to emphasize a set of dogmatic beliefs. Correct belief took the place of concrete action. This change resulted (1) partly from identifying faith with a set of doctrines; (2) partly from the bitter quarrels after

Luther's death; and (3) partly from the Peace of Augsburg. (The Peace of Augsburg in 1555 was the attempt to settle the religious problem in Germany by giving each prince the right to decide whether Lutheranism or Catholicism would be the religion of the people within his territory.)

Toward the end of the seventeenth century Lutheranism had become formal and staid. Luther's warmth and his emphasis on love as an expression of faith had virtually been lost. Right belief predominated the joy and gratitude that Luther felt in doing good works because of what God had done for him. The ruling authorities had taken the priesthood of all believers to mean that they should control the church. Bureaucratic corruption resulted.

Out of this background arose pietism. Evangelical pietism began when Philip Spener (pronounced *SPAY-ner*), a Lutheran pastor, sought to find a more satisfying personal religion. The lifeless forms into which the Lutheran state church had sunk were inadequate. Spener's search led to a revival of spiritual heart-warming fervor in Protestantism. To revive committed Christian living, he urged laymen to study the Bible, to pray, and to take Luther's priesthood of all believers seriously, for, he said, it applied to them. Small groups of Christians began meeting in his home. The movement spread. A small book by Spener published in 1675 became a best seller. In it Spener told about the corrupt conditions of the church and how they could be corrected. Many in the established state-church were enraged. Many felt threatened.

Spener's disciples, particularly A. H. Francke, introduced pietism (with its emphasis on feelings as a guide to religious truth) into the universities. The University of Halle rapidly became a thriving center for the new movement. Over the years thousands of pastors for Germany got their training there. Even so, the movement was not accepted in Lutheran circles. It might have died out except for Count Zinzendorf who became the spiritual leader of the Moravians at Herrnhut. Through the Moravians, pietism passed directly to John Wesley and the Methodists. (S/R, 53.)

John Wesley first encountered the Moravians on board ship when he came to America. In the midst of a storm at sea, when Wesley was terrified because he thought the ship would sink, the Moravians prayed and sang hymns. They seemed joyful, quite undisturbed by the crashing waves and howling winds. In Savannah, Georgia, Spangenberg (the Moravian pastor) asked Wesley if he knew Christ as his Savior. Wesley stumbled over some answers, and then said yes, only to admit later that he lied. He felt no such thing in his heart. The Moravians, particularly Peter Böhler, led Wesley to his Aldersgate Street experience when he felt his heart strangely warmed. This experience was Wesley's way of knowing the truth about Christ and God. Wesley made several trips to Herrnhut in Germany and translated many of the Moravian hymns into English.

The hymns of the Methodists afforded an opportunity for the expression of personal convictions and feelings such as had not been experienced in England for centuries. The fervor with which thousands sang the Methodist hymns indicated how starved they were for this kind of feeling and emotion in religion. (S/R, 54.)

But is emotional feeling enough? No. Feeling alone is not a sound basis on which to make judgments. Anyone knows from experience how difficult it is to make balanced decisions in the midst of hate, anger, or joy. And strangely enough, too much emphasis on feeling and not enough on reason was one of the great weaknesses of the entire pietistic movement. In spite of the fact that the University of Halle was a center for pietism and in spite of the fact that later pietists did establish schools, still the pietists generally neglected intellectual pursuits. Pietism squeezed religion into a narrow mold. Feeling became the all-important factor. This carried over into the great revivals of the eighteenth century in this country.

■ Scan again the preceding section dealing with pietism. Then let one person read aloud *S/R*, 53 as others listen.

To discover something of the influence of pietism on Protestantism—in particular, on Methodism—practice identifying the pietistic orientation of your class.

Let each person write a brief personal statement of faith. Now each person will look at the statement for evidences of pietism as described in *S/R*, 53. To what extent has pietism influenced your statement of faith?

Or the entire class might examine some familiar hymns for evidence of pietistic influence. What words and phrases in the hymns describe the ideas and attitudes set forth in *S/R*, 53?

Discuss: What, in your opinion, is the importance of individual salvation over against the salvation of society? See *S/R*, 29; begin with paragraph eight and end with paragraph seventeen.

■ Dependence on feeling as evidence of truth has been and still is prevalent among Methodists. Yet, feeling alone is not a sound basis on which to make judgments. For example, when John Wesley's experience of the "warm heart" began to dissipate, he became uncertain that he was saved. See *S/R*, 75. What are other criteria by which to judge?

Divide the class into four small groups. If the class is large, more than one group may deal with the same issue or you may select others. Each group should choose one of the following situations about which they will ask the questions: As a Christian what data do you need in addition to feeling? What data would you secure in trying to carry out your Christian commitment to truth?

Group A—taking a new job
Group B—supporting a political candidate
Group C—disciplining a child
Group D—contemplating divorce

A reporter may summarize the findings of the group for the entire class.

I BELIEVE BECAUSE THE CHURCH TEACHES

Americans have a history of rebellion against authority in any form. This dislike of "being told" extends to religious authority as well. American Christians have never felt they had to stick too closely to what someone else said they must believe. This has certainly been true since the failure of the early Puritan commonwealth to maintain an iron hand on religious opinions.

The most authoritarian of all religious bodies in America

is the Roman Catholic Church. This church has always shown a rigorous attitude toward dissent. The climax of this authoritarianism came, however, in the nineteenth century in two decisions, the first by Pope Pius IX in 1864 and the second in 1870 by the first Vatican Council.

In modern Catholicism, the necessity to believe exactly what the church teaches without any dissent whatsoever goes back to the Council of Trent. In 1563, several dogmatic decrees were set forth by the council. (A dogmatic decree is an official view put forth by Catholic authority and *must be believed* by every member of that church.) The Council of Trent was held to counter the Reformation begun by Martin Luther. The decrees of that council reasserted the central doctrines of Catholicism intended to stamp out the "heresies" of Reformation. Catholics were told what they *must* believe about the Scriptures, original sin, justification, the sacraments, and the like.

Another dogmatic decree of modern Catholicism came about three hundred years later. On December 8, 1854, Pope Pius IX put forth a decree that the Virgin Mary had not inherited original sin as had all other mortals. This doctine, called the Immaculate Conception, is a required article of faith for Catholics.

Exactly ten years later, on December 8, 1864, Pope Pius IX issued a document on his own authority to all Catholics. This document was called *The Papal Syllabus of Errors.* It is negative in form and condemns viewpoints contrary to the Catholic view of truth. Catholics could not believe, for instance, that "every man [is] free to embrace and profess the religion he shall believe true, guided by the light of reason." No Catholic could believe that "Protestantism is nothing more than another form of the same true Christian religion, in which it is possible to be equally pleasing to God as in the Catholic Church." Eighty errors were set forth in this decree.

Another dogmatic decree came in 1870 in which the first Vatican Council set forth the necessity of Catholics to believe that when the pope speaks as the "pastor and doctor of all Christians" and "defines a doctrine regarding faith or morals to be held by the universal church" he is infallible. That is, the pope cannot be in error when he is speaking officially for the church, when he defines what other Catholics must believe. (S/R, 55.)

At the opposite extreme from this authoritarian view is the Methodist tradition. Printed in our *Discipline* are the twenty-five Articles of Religion which are regarded as one of the standards of doctrine of the church. The exact authority of these articles does not arise, however, when a person takes the vows of membership. The baptismal vows ask about belief in God and Jesus Christ, but go no further in required beliefs. John Wesley himself did not require that all members of the societies hold his views. (S/R, 56.)

■ Let two persons read aloud *S/R,* 55 and 56. Then, let the whole group compare the attitude toward authority set forth in each of the readings. At what points or in what situations are the teachings of the church authoritative for you? Why do you or why do you not accept for yourself the authority of the Articles of Religion or the Social Creed of the Methodist Church?

I BELIEVE BECAUSE THE BIBLE SAYS SO

Some people look upon whatever the church or the Bible says as final. This may seem to afford certainty and security, but it hardly encourages thinking. Further, most divisions in the church have arisen over differences of interpretation. Persons disagree over exactly what the Bible teaches. "Because the Bible says so" may not always be so simple to discover. As an illustration, take the various interpretations of the verses in the Bible on baptism. How diverse are the views of the churches on baptism, yet every church thinks it is true to what "the Bible says" about baptism. "What the Bible says" requires more than finding all the verses in the Scriptures dealing with a particular theme. It involves the study of commentaries and other reference books and, most

important of all, the guidance of the Holy Spirit to understand in fact and spirit "what the Bible says."

In the same category could be placed those who say they
believe because of the way that they were brought up. Religion then becomes mixed with the mores of a particular
country or region. (S/R, 57.) It enables people to relate
well with those about them, but it shuts them off from the
greater testimony of world Christianity.

■ What beliefs do people say they hold because they are in the
Bible? As the members of the class suggest some, let one person
list them on newsprint or chalkboard. Discuss: How do you decide
on what matters you let the Bible be your final authority?

■ Use one of the "Six Conversations" (Resource Packet, *God
With Us*, item 3) at this point. The Leaders' Guide in that packet
contains instructions as well as questions for discussion.

I BELIEVE BECAUSE IT HAS BEEN REVEALED TO ME

Many people have believed in direct revelation, and who
can say whether or not a person has received a revelation?
In the time of the Reformation, Martin Luther tested revelations by whether or not they conformed to the revealed Word
in the Bible. He assumed that since the Spirit was claimed
as the source of the revelations and since the Spirit was the
author of the Bible, there could be no contradiction between
the two. Anything not in the Bible was suspected as an in-
novation.

Claims of direct inspiration have continued in Christian
circles. Sometimes the results have been exemplary, sometimes ludicrous. George Fox, founder of the Quakers, on a
direct "command" from God left his relatives in 1643 and
began his wanderings in England. He received an "opening"
from the Lord to forsake priests and dissenters and to follow
the leading of the Inner Light. Convinced through the Inner
Light of the brotherhood and equality of all men, Fox would
not remove his hat in the presence of dignitaries, addressed
the king of England by his first name, refused to bow to

royalty, declined to wear fancy clothes, and dared in an age of cruelty and brutality not to use violence. He stood staunchly against war, slavery, sham, formalism, and wantonness. He rejected the sacraments and formal religion saying that one should wait in silence for the leading of the Spirit.

In the Massachusetts Bay Colony, Anne Hutchinson was not a Quaker but she did believe in the immediate inspiration of the Spirit. The ministers of the Boston area reacted angrily when she said all of them with the exception of her own minister, John Cotton, were preaching more works than grace. People met in her home to voice their criticisms. Since the church and state were bound together in a holy experiment, her attacks were too much to be tolerated. She threatened the biblical basis of the government. After several of her friends had been exiled, she was brought to trial in 1637, and trapped into declaring her immediate inspiration. She was certain of what she was doing in the same way that Abraham was certain that he should not sacrifice his own son— by immediate revelation. This was contrary to interpretation of the Bible through the established ministry. It would undermine the government. So Anne Hutchinson was banished.

■ Listen as three persons read aloud the playlet "Anne Hutchinson" (Resource Packet, item 3) . See the Leaders' Guide in the packet for questions and suggestions. What is the understanding of the force of the individual conscience held by those involved in the incident? Do you believe that people still receive special direction or guidance today? Contrast the view of divine guidance in the dialogue with the view of divine guidance that has social consequences, such as the man who burns himself to death to protest a situation. What criteria do you use for evaluating the two?

■ Let the members of the group share experiences of times when they have received personal guidance, such as direction to perform a certain act; or assurance about changing jobs.

■ Perhaps some members of your class can visit a Quaker meeting and report their visit to the class.

I BELIEVE IN REASON

You may be thinking, "I believe only if it is reasonable." This stance is a historic one that became widely accepted in the seventeenth and eighteenth centuries with the rise of rationalism and science. Reason is a gift from God which men should use as they do other gifts. Reason has played a significant role in Christianity. Men like Augustine, Luther, Pascal, and Barth did not become leaders in Christianity without careful use of rational thought. It is also a fact, however, that almost all the great leaders in Christianity have disparaged reason. Luther denounced it as a safe guide. So, the question arises, "Why?" Shouldn't Christians use reason?

Reason began to dominate the outlook of Western man in the seventeenth century, and the church was largely responsible for bringing it about. Men had grown tired of hundreds of years of religious strife, witch burning, heretic hunting, inquisitorial racks, and wholesale slaughter. Such things did not seem to be in keeping with the Christ of the Gospels. By what authority did church officials, whether Catholic or Protestant, say something was a revealed truth for which men should be put to death?

This new attitude came at a time when science was beginning its modern development. Science and reason teamed up. Although Galileo, one of the great scientists of the time, was accused of heresy and forced to recant, it was the last great "success" of the church in suppressing science.

The discoveries of science led men to believe that the world is a grand mechanism with constant laws which man can discover and use. Revealed religion seemed to be out of it. Descartes (pronounced *day-CART*), provided the motto for the new age: *All conceptions must be doubted until adequately demonstrated, and adequate proof must have the certainty of mathematics.*

A group of men known as romanticists pointed out that emotion also has a place in human life and belief. Some aspects of life elude the analysis of reason. Truth may be found through inner voices, intuition, feeling, and love. Mystery, beauty, and impulses defy the processes of reason, yet much depends on them. Reason failed to order life neatly. The destructiveness of the French Revolution revealed this more than anything else.

In trying to decide what is truth, however, man is not to throw reason to the winds, nor must he follow it to the exclusion of everything else. The former is as ridiculous as the latter is idolatrous. Reason is one of the gifts of God to be used along with the other marvelous gifts bestowed on man.

What is truth? Each man must finally decide for himself and live accordingly. How can the church help in the search for truth in our time? (*S/R,* 58.)

■ Have a panel composed of persons representing several different disciplines (educator, scientist, musician, economist). In all of life, we have to use reason after we have made faith commitments. These faith commitments are working assumptions that cannot be proved and we make them in every phase of life, not only the "religious." Let the panel discuss this question: How do we use reason in making decisions related to all areas of our work? Have I ever received any support or help from the church in my search for truth regarding such matters? What does it mean to have any kind of faith on the basis of this chapter? How is faith appropriate to any decision? To any discipline?

■ You might close this session by reading aloud one of the scriptural references listed at the beginning of this chapter, or let members of the class read silently *S/R,* 58.

■ Let the leadership team be prepared to give assignments for the next chapter of study and the members of the group be prepared to accept the assignments.

Read these selections in your Bible:
Ecclesiastes 3:1-8
A time for everything.

Philippians 3:8-16
Pressing forward.

9

□□

CAN THE CHURCH SURVIVE CHANGE?

We hear much talk today about the church as an agent of change. To say that the church should become a change agent is to admit that things are not as they should be and that the church should take the lead in changing them.

This attitude toward change raises a whole series of questions about our heritage and may give us some clues to the future. Why does the church resist change? Has the church ever fostered change? Can the church survive change? How can the church keep the old values and be open to the new? Must the church always be conservative? What out of the past should be preserved?

Many people feel they cannot plan for the future. Things important now will be out-of-date within a few years. The director of psychiatry at the University of Wisconsin in an

■ *As you arrive at your place of meeting, check the assignment chart for specific preparation to be made before the session begins.*
■ *Set goals for your study of this chapter as suggested on page 15.*

article in *Think* pointed to the inability of young people to absorb so much change. This, he said, is the chief cause of dissent and insecurity which we see in hippies and teeny-boopers. What does this mean for the church? "How has the church responded to change?" is a particularly important question for us today. (*S/R*, 59.)

■ This chapter examines the response of the church to change at various stages in her history. At this point divide the class into at least five groups. Groups should not exceed six persons. If your class is large, more than one group may be assigned the same task. Each group will study one section of this chapter.

    Group A—Early Christianity
    Group B—Change in the Middle Ages
    Group C—Response to Change in Catholicism
    Group D—Response to Change in Protestantism: Fundamentalism
    Group E—Response to Change in Protestantism: Liberalism

    Let each group select some of these questions to guide its study: What changes or conditions in society caused the church to respond? How did the church respond? How did the church in this period evidence resistance to change? What were the results of the church's response to change? How would you evaluate the response of the church? In what ways are we experiencing today the results of the church's response in that period? Consider also the selected readings suggested with each section. Allow time for a reporter from each group to share a brief summary of the group's ideas with the entire class.

EARLY CHRISTIANITY

Change is not foreign to Christianity. It came into existence because a small group dared to believe the Resurrection. Despite Rome's crucifixion of Jesus as an insurrectionist and the Jews' denunciation of him as a blasphemer, early believers hailed Christ as the foretold Messiah. When John's disciples asked who he was, Jesus said: "Go and tell John what you hear and see: the blind receive their sight and the lame walk, lepers are cleansed and the deaf hear, and the dead are raised up, and the poor have good news preached to them" (Matthew 11:4-5).

Everything that Jesus did pointed to change. He criticized the Pharisees, Sadduccees, and scribes for their hypocrisy and pride. He drove the money-changers from the Temple. (Matthew 21:12-13.) He told the disciple who would first bury his father to let the dead bury their dead. (Matthew 8:21-22.) He commanded his followers to return good for evil, to go a second mile if forced to go one mile, to seek righteousness before the things of this world. (Matthew 5:38-42; 6: 25:33.) Despite old laws, he healed a man on the sabbath. (Matthew 12:9-13.) He proclaimed, "I and the Father are one." (John 10:30.) He could have had all the pomp and glory of all the kingdoms on earth, yet he willed to live and die through love. He let himself be crucified on a cross that he might draw all men to himself through love. The Resurrection vindicated his promises that in him all things would be made new.

Christianity virtually exploded on the Roman world. No one seemed to know what to do with the "superstitious" followers of Christ. The Romans branded them as dangerous enemies of society, a threat to the cult of emperor worship, traitors who ought to be thrown to the lions and gored to death by wild bulls. For 250 years they were hounded, persecuted, and martyred. They did not gain full, official acceptance until Constantine's edict of toleration in 313. Then their influence was such in the Roman Empire that by 380 Christianity became the *only* legal religion in the Roman Empire.

This change from a formerly persecuted church to the only legal religion in the Roman Empire came in less than seventy years. Not everybody, however, considered the change good. Christianity had become a state religion, accepting favors and in turn bestowing sanctions. The church became worldly. Throughout the Middle Ages the church and state vied with one another for worldly power. For 1,300 years church and state struggled to see which would dominate the union of the two. Each produced its champions. Neither emerged as victor until nationalism predominated in the seventeenth century.

CHANGE IN THE MIDDLE AGES

Immediately after the time of Constantine, in reaction to the worldliness of the church, laymen by the thousands withdrew to the wilds of the deserts and the mountains. There they hoped to live the Christian life in solitude, away from the distractions of civilization. Somewhat surprisingly, the monastic movement became the bearer of civilization in the dark periods of the Middle Ages. When the barbarians overran the Roman Empire, the church was forced to become rural and self-sustaining. Support from Rome was not possible; the usual lines of commerce and communication broke down. Paris, London, and Rome became small villages. The self-contained monasteries then became islands of learning, hospitals, and hostels in a culture that seemed to be disintegrating.

The same story could be repeated with regard to missions throughout the history of Christianity. Missionaries have penetrated strange and even hostile countries. Changed conditions challenged them to greater effort.

RECENT RESPONSE TO CHANGE

Certainly change has not been foreign to Christianity. Again and again changed conditions have simply presented the church with new opportunities. But the image of the church as an institution that resists change persists. Persons devoted to the King James Bible burned copies of the Revised Standard Version when it appeared in the 1940's. They did not want any modernization of the wording of the translation that appeared in 1611, despite the fact that the meanings of many words had changed. Anyone who has worked in a church for any length of time knows the force of the argument, "We have always done it this way."

Anyone who has followed the struggle for civil rights for all Americans knows that the churches resisted taking positive action on equal opportunities for Mexicans, Indians, and Negroes. Martin Luther King's letter from a Birmingham

137

jail is a masterpiece of holy indignation against those church-men who wanted to wait, to go slow, to take it easy. (*S/R*, 60.) The churches of America, with the exception of the Roman Catholic Church, generally resisted the unionizing of labor at the turn into the twentieth century. The coming of the unions was one of the major changes in our recent culture. In England, William Booth—founder of the Salvation Army—discovered that the churches of London would not accept the drunks and paupers that he was netting at the sewers. As Protestant churches in America lost interest in the working man and became middle class churches, they defended middle and upper-class values.

■ Divide the class into groups of four or five persons. Let each group decide upon a situation that affirms the claim either that the church as an institution *resists* change or that the church as an institution *encourages* change. As time allows let persons selected by the groups present the situations in role plays (a spontaneous acting out of a situation). Remember that in role playing the problem or situation is gotten out into the open but no solution is offered. After the groups have presented their situations, let the members of the other groups suggest ways they think the church might or should respond.

■ Conduct an opinion poll. Let each person write on a 3x5 card what he considers to be the three most crucial local situations to which your church should respond. Collect the cards and have one member of the class list the items on newsprint or chalkboard for easy viewing by members of the group.

Brainstorm (offering of spontaneous ideas) for one minute all the ways you think the church should respond to each situation listed. One person should write the ideas on newsprint or chalkboard as they are offered. A procedure at the end of this chapter will call for discussion of the list.

Discuss: What changes might be required in our attitudes in order to take such steps? What changes in the social, racial, political, and economic life of your community could you expect if the church responded as you suggest?

RESPONSE TO CHANGE IN CATHOLICISM

In 1954 the Catholics made a saint of Pius X, who had been pope from 1903 to 1914. His pontificate was ultraconservative and reactionary—conservative in that he upheld the traditional doctrines of Catholicism, and reactionary in that his pronouncements condemned modern twentieth-century trends. In 1907 he specifically enumerated sixty-five errors of "modernism." In 1910 he issued an Oath Against Modernism requiring priests and teachers to swear that the church's teachings are inerrant at whatever points they conflict with the errors of this age. Those who refused to sign were no longer considered teachers. In 1931 the Oath was extended to laymen and clerics at Catholic universities.

The canonization of Pius X took place just nine years before Vatican Council II (1963-65). In effect it sanctioned four hundred years of ultraconservatism. Vatican II is significant precisely because it looks as if it has turned back that long tradition of antimodernism.

Although Vatican II has altered very few doctrines, it has greatly changed the atmosphere in Catholicism. Priests can now hold discussions with clergymen from other churches, even worship with them. Catholics are singing Luther's "A Mighty Fortress Is Our God," and some Dutch groups are taking communion with Protestants. For four hundred years this was virtually impossible in Catholicism. (S/R, 61.)

The Catholic stand against modernism illustrates how institutions as well as individuals sometimes react to shocks. The shocks that caused Catholicism to react were the Protestant Reformation and the French Revolution. Both of them threatened the historic claims of the Catholic Church, and Rome reacted by voicing its claims even more strongly.

In reaction to the Protestant Reformation, the Catholics framed the doctrines of the Council of Trent (1545-63). After this council, no other council was needed in Catholicism until Pope Pius IX called Vatican Council I in 1869. It was this council that pronounced the dogma of papal infallibility. (See Chapter 8 in this book.) The Council of Trent developed the basic attitude of Catholicism toward the major problems of the church in society. It declared that the church is superior to all secular authorities; it placed tradition on a par with Scripture and made the pope the final interpreter of both. The Council of Trent said justification is a matter of God and man working together, exalted celibacy and virginity above marriage, put marriage under the control of the church, declared the Apocrypha is part of the canonized Bible which everyone must believe, and adopted Jerome's Vulgate Latin translation as the official version of the Bible. This council also confirmed the seven sacraments, reasserted transubstantiation and withholding of the communion cup from the laity, continued asking the help of the saints and continued masses for the dead, approved the censoring of books, and repeatedly damned the views of the Protestants.

For a while, just before the French Revolution, it looked as if Catholicism would change its stance. In 1773 the pope dissolved the powerful militant arm of the church—the Jesuits—as the Society of Jesus was called. The Society was founded by Ignatius Loyola. It received papal sanction in 1540. Its members were sworn to obey the pope and to do anything to promote the church. They agreed to say white was black if it would promote the church. A doctrine of "mental reservation" permitted them to withhold truth or to leave a false impression if the church could be promoted thereby. The special fields of the Jesuits were missions and education, in both of which they were phenomenally successful. The Jesuits grew so strong that the pope dissolved the Society in 1773.

Then in 1789 the French Revolution erupted, followed by the dictatorship of Napoleon. Napoleon imprisoned the pope for five years. He treated the pope as if he were another ordinary citizen. In the French Revolution the papacy saw what one could expect from such modern ideas as liberty, equality, and fraternity, and the worship of reason. The papacy chose to maintain the secure, stable truths of the past. In 1814, the pope re-established the Jesuits. The act sym-

140

bolized the stance from which the papacy would not budge.

If one wonders why some Catholic priests like Father James Kavanaugh have criticized their church as medieval when it comes to views on sex, birth control, education, civic clubs, liturgy, censoring of books, and standards for movies, the answer is clear. (S/R, 62.)

In the nineteenth and twentieth centuries the Roman Church has repeatedly smashed its liberal voices—Lamennais, Tyrrell, Loisy, Teilhard de Chardin, and many others. On the other hand, it has repeatedly pronounced its official stand against all modernism. In the revolutionary attempts to unify Italy and in the rise of Darwinism, the papacy saw ideas similar to those that resulted in the French Revolution. As we noticed in the preceding chapter, in 1864 Pope Pius IX issued his *Syllabus of Errors,* a declaration of war on all forms of modernism—pantheism, naturalism, absolute rationalism, freedom of worship, toleration of all religions, socialism, secret societies, Bible societies, free masonry, and separation of church and state. He even condemned the idea that "the Roman Pontiff can and ought to reconcile himself to, and agree with, progress, liberalism, and civilization as lately introduced." In 1870 Pope Pius IX maneuvered the dogma of papal infallibility through Vatican Council I. The pope controlled the committees, determined the agenda, approved all motions, and counted the votes. Many Roman Catholic leaders were dismayed. Some Catholics who were dissatisfied withdrew to form the Old Catholic Church.

Following Pius IX came Pope Leo XIII (1878-1903). He recognized a changed situation in Western culture, but he reaffirmed the ideas of the Council of Trent. He decreed the study of the medieval master Thomas Aquinas for all clerics and scholars; accepted toleration of other religions not as something good but as expedient in the light of current circumstances; pronounced against freedom of worship, press, conscience, and teaching; established a Biblical Commission to deal with wayward biblical scholars; and stated

141

again the superiority of the church over all other institutions which by divine right the papacy should control.

Thus Roman Catholicism came into the twentieth century armed with an arsenal to repulse all modernism. In 1928 it rejected all ecumenical endeavors except those that would bring everybody back to Rome; and in 1950 it rebuffed a growing sense of ecumenicity by announcing the bodily ascension of Mary into heaven. Nothing could have been more calculated to infuriate Protestants.

Nevertheless new vistas did begin to appear in Roman Catholicism. Bishops from around the world felt that the church was losing contact with modern society. They demanded to be heard. At Vatican II they were heard. In Pope John XXIII they found a champion. John added "St. Joseph" to one of the prayers of the mass to show that the ancient canon *could* be changed. When Vatican II convened, for the first time in the history of ecumenical councils it addressed its opening remarks to "all men," thus symbolizing the new outreach of the church. Roman Catholicism is more open to change today than it has been for 400 years.

RESPONSE TO CHANGE IN PROTESTANTISM

Should Christians hold to the old, regardless? How can one know which changes are good and which are not?

Fundamentalism. Some thought in the middle of the nineteenth century that the time was ripe for a new religion —a religion of humanity, a religion in which love of humanity would replace the love of God. Auguste Comte, a French sociologist, believed the relief of human needs was more important than striving to get to heaven. For Comte the old religious views had outlived their usefulness. (Some of his intellectual descendants in 1933, a hundred years later, signed the *Humanist Manifesto*. They declared that the time had passed for belief in God and called on men to work simply for the betterment of humanity. Science has the answers. Man has no future life, only the present. Hence, man must work passionately to improve this life.)

An even heavier blow to literalism seemed to come with the publication of Charles Darwin's *On the Origin of Species* in 1859 and *The Descent of Man* in 1871. Darwin theorized, on the basis of convincing evidence, that all of life developed from lower forms by an evolutionary process of natural selection. (*S/R*, 63.) This bold theory seemed to discredit the account of spontaneous creation found in Genesis. But more than that, Christians applied a form of evolution to the Bible and came up with historical form criticism. The Bible was not dictated by God; it had evolved out of the religious life of the Hebrews. Scholars in Europe and America probed the Bible with the same literary and historical standards applied to the study of any other book. Of particular biblical passages they asked who wrote them, when, why, and for whom. They argued that the Scriptures were the human products of their own times, far from perfect, that Moses did not write the first five books of the Bible, that David did not write all the psalms, that Paul could not be the author of all the letters attributed to him, and that the Virgin Birth did not conform to science or reason.

One response to the rapid changes in America (not just in religion but in almost every area of life) in the early years of this century was fundamentalism. Fundamentalism was a response to changes that shaped Western culture in the nineteenth and twentieth centuries. These changes centered in developments about reason and science. Although Scripture and right reason were the twin authorities established by the Reformation, the fundamentalists believed that the increased appeal to reason was drawing Christianity further and further away from its scriptural bases.

Many people, including some scientists, felt that Christianity had been struck a series of fatal blows by the new theories. The authority of the Bible had been slowly whittled away, they thought. In 1895 at a convention of religious conservatives in New York, the famous five fundamentals were adopted: the inerrancy of the Bible, the divinity of Jesus Christ, the substitutionary atonement of Christ through the cross, the physical resurrection, and Christ's second coming.

After publication in 1910 of a series of pamphlets under the title of *The Fundamentals,* in which these doctrines were set forth as the standard of Christian belief, those who followed this point of view became known as the "fundamentalists." (*S/R,* 64.) (Sometimes the term is mistakenly applied to all religious conservatives.) If a person did not literally believe in all five of these fundamentals, he was not a Christian and should not be admitted to the church. Since God cannot contradict himself, they said, man's approach to the Bible must be faulty. As a result of fundamentalist pressure, Tennessee passed a law prohibiting the teaching of evolution in the public schools, resulting in the dramatic trial of John T. Scopes in 1925. (The Tennessee law against the teaching of evolution was not repealed until 1967.)

Toward the end of the nineteenth century and the beginning of the twentieth, powerful evangelists rose up to defend the "old time religion." Dwight L. Moody, a businessman, expanded a Sunday school class into a world-wide evangelistic movement. He interpreted the Bible literally and conducted massive Bible conferences, prayer meetings, and revivals in America and Europe. Thousands joined the ranks of Christianity under his spellbinding sermons. His English counterpart was Henry Drummond whose sermon on First Corinthians 13, "The Greatest Thing in the World," typifies an individualistic piety that is often associated with fundamentalism. Billy Sunday and many others followed. In Great Britain more than 137,000 laymen and ministers signed petitions attesting their belief in divine inspiration and future punishment in hell. In America many clergymen lost their pulpits for not believing in the Virgin Birth. The fundamen-

talists believed that reason would destroy the Bible, that it
would lead to skepticism, relativism, and nihilism.

■ Have a panel of four persons (one person will act as moderator),
notified in advance, discuss the questions raised at the beginning
of this chapter: Why does the church resist change? How can the
church keep the old values but be open to the new? What out of
the church's past should be preserved? How can the church initiate
change? How can the church survive change? If the church does not
change, will it soon find itself irrelevant and out of date? The
questions should be considered in the light of S/R, 59, 60, 61, and
62 and pages 135-47 of this chapter. News items from recent newspapers, periodicals, and secular magazines might also provide perti-
nent information. What do Ecclesiastes 3:1-8 and Philippians 3:
8-16 say to these questions?

Let a second group of four persons form a reactant panel. Each
person will react (respond) to the ideas and statements of one
particular member of the first panel.

■ Use the "Chart of Key Questions" (Resource Packet, item 4) to
guide your study of the church's response to change. See the Leaders'
Guide in the packet for detailed instructions.

Liberalism. The liberals felt that truth and progress were
at stake. They believed that the fundamentalists had over-
reacted. They believed that reason is a gift of God that man
should use and that God's inspiration is not necessarily limited to the Bible. Reason is the instrument that man was commanded to use to gain dominion over the earth. The Bible
does have inconsistencies; it is the product of imperfect men,
as Paul admits in 2 Corinthians 4:7. The liberals did not
think they were sacrificing biblical truth, but reinterpreting
it and applying it to modern times. Evolution was but God's
providence at work in the world. (S/R, 65.) William H.
Carruth summarized a whole era in his memorable poem,
"Each in His Own Tongue":

> A fire-mist and a planet,
>   A crystal and a cell,
> A jellyfish and a saurian,
>   And caves where the cavemen dwell;
> Then a sense of law and beauty,
>   And a face turned from the clod—
> Some call it Evolution,
>   And others call it God.*

145

■ Some persons have said that the Protestant Reformation sub-
stituted a "paper pope" (the Bible) for a pope at Rome.

Have three persons read aloud *S/R*, 44, 55, and 65. Members of
the class will want to follow each reading carefully.

Form groups of four to six persons. On the basis of the selected
readings, discuss these questions: In what ways are fundamentalist
attitudes toward the Bible like the Roman Catholic view of papal
infallibility? Unlike? Catholics believe that the pope and the church
are divinely inspired and that God will not let me make a mistake.
How does this view compare with the belief in an infallible book?

Men like Walter Rauschenbusch (pronounced *ROW-
shen-BUSH*) believed that the individualistic piety of fundamentalism was not a sufficient understanding of the gospel.
They felt Christ was calling men to correct the ills of society.
Men must work on a large scale to improve working conditions, eliminate slums, stamp out disease, increase education,
and stop economic injustices. (*S/R*, 66.) Rauschenbusch
worked incessantly for a social gospel, and the social gospel
became a hallmark of liberalism. Out of this period of church
history (1900-1912) came most of the social creeds of the
American churches.

For some liberals, sin could be overcome with education
and better living conditions. A belief in the perfectibility
of man prevailed, if not in the classical sense of perfection,
then at least in John Wesley's sense: a redeemed man will
not know everything and he will make mistakes, but he can
act in love and not deliberately commit injustices. The belief in man as a depraved, sinful creature was pushed into
the background along with the old doctrine of predestina-
tion.

In 1933 Henry P. Van Dusen named five basic presupposi-
tions of liberalism: devotion to truth, deference to science
and the scientific method, doubt about man's attaining final
truth, the interrelatedness of everything, and confidence in
human reason and tolerance. Harry Emerson Fosdick, a symbol of liberalism in the 1920's and 30's, hailed man's ability
to make progress through the conquest of ignorance, sin,

apathy, and inefficiency. He welcomed change and free inquiry. He summoned Christians to usher in the kingdom of God by setting aside prescientific notions and dealing with the religious needs of men in a scientific age. He wanted Christians "to think the great faiths of the Gospel through in contemporary terms, and to harness the great dynamics of the Gospel to contemporary tasks. . . . If that be heresy, the orthodox will have to make the most of it." When Fosdick was attacked for his views, he left the Presbyterian Church. John D. Rockefeller, Jr., built Riverside Church in New York City and Fosdick had a distinguished ministry there.

The theological differences of the early years of the century are still found among Methodists. It is not essential that all Methodists hold to the same interpretations of religious beliefs beyond the essentials found in baptismal and membership vows. (See again S/R, 56.)

This chapter has given only a glimpse of how the church has responded to change. Obviously, no response has been crystal clear and perfect. Man must have the courage of his convictions and not be swayed by every "new" claim. Yet man must have the courage to risk change lest his witness become irrelevant, for the world does change. No man's views are final; none infallible; because man is not God.

HOW TO EVALUATE CHANGE

How can we evaluate change so that we will have some guidelines for acting? There is no set formula or standard that will always apply, but certain questions may serve as guides: What gains and losses do we see in the responses that people made in the past to similar situations? Will *my* contemplated response to change benefit people? What will my response indicate about my true belief in God and my relationship to other persons? Is my stand subtly serving myself to the detriment of others? Are hidden motives directing my response? What light does the Bible cast on the situation? Will my response affirm or deny life? What would be the result if all men chose to respond in the same way as I?

■ It is difficult to determine when change is good and when it is not. Listed above are several questions that might be used as guidelines for acting in the midst of change. Use these questions to evaluate your list of possible responses of the church suggested during the brainstorming. How relevant and valuable are these questions for you in your situation? What additional criteria would you suggest for evaluating change?

■ The session might be closed with silent prayer.

■ Let the leadership team be prepared to give assignments for the next chapter of study and the members of the group be prepared to accept the assignments.

NOTES ON CHAPTER 9

Page 145: In *The World's Greatest Religious Poetry,* edited by Caroline Miles Hill (Macmillan Company, 1939), page 145. Used by permission.

Read these selections in your Bible:
Matthew 28:19-20
The great command.

John 17:1-26
Christ's prayer for unity.

Ephesians 2:11-22
Living in Christ.

10
□□

SHOULD THE CHURCHES UNITE?

Abraham Lincoln never joined the church. His reason has some significance for us when we think about the divisions among the churches. Here is what he said:

> I have never united myself to any church, because I have found difficulty in giving my assent, without mental reservation, to the long, complicated statements of Christian doctrine which characterize their articles of belief and confessions of faith. When any church will inscribe over its altars, as its sole qualification for membership, the Savior's condensed statement of the substance of both law and gospel, "Thou shalt love the Lord thy God with all thy heart, and with all thy soul, and with all thy mind, and thy neighbor as thyself," that church will I join with all my heart and all my soul.*

In spite of the fact that many persons in the denominations would agree that Lincoln's creed would be sufficient for

■ *As you arrive at your place of meeting, check the assignment chart for specific preparation to be made before the session begins.*
■ *Set goals for your study of this chapter as suggested on page 15.*

149

them, some would rather "see the roof fall in" than join with other Christians in church union.

In spite of the attitude of many Christians who would rather "see the roof fall in" than unite with others, the talk of church union among the denominations has never been stronger. The United Methodist Church of 1968 is a product of the union of The Methodist Church and The Evangelical United Brethren Church. The Methodist Church was formed in 1939 in a union of the Methodist Episcopal Church, the Methodist Protestant Church and the Methodist Episcopal Church, South. The Evangelical United Brethren Church was a result of union in 1946 of the Evangelical and the United Brethren churches. The United Methodist Church is today made up of churchmen who were in five separate churches in 1939. (S/R, 67.)

Proposals have been made in recent years that would unite the major Protestant bodies of the United States into a church of more than twenty million members. The Methodist Church and The Evangelical United Brethren Church were both invited to be a part of this union.

So questions are being raised. Why is there a movement toward unity? Is it desirable? What precisely is at stake? How will it affect me? What will I have to give up? What will I gain? Will unity mean the same kind of worship for everybody? These are not idle questions. They point to the concern of the ordinary Christian.

■ Each person should have a 3x5 card and a pencil. Individually, think about and list: the five persons with whom you are presently working on projects, like urban renewal, hospital volunteer work, or open housing; the five persons with whom you feel freest to be yourself; and the five persons to whom you would turn for advice about a personal or family problem.

Now, look at the names you have listed, how many are members of other denominations? Does denomination make any difference to you? Is there any relation between the acceptance or rejection of persons and unity among churches? What prohibits the union between your church and another church in your community? What basis would make it possible? Talk with another person for a few minutes about your insights and conclusions.

Then, in groups of six to eight persons discuss the question: What is the basis of church unity? Read John 17 and *S/R,* 68. What does theological confrontation involve? Does confrontation tend to be uniting or dividing? Why?

THE SPLIT BETWEEN EAST AND WEST

The movement toward unity has many causes. (The movement toward unity is called the "ecumenical [pronounced *EKK-you-MEN-i-kal*] movement," from the Greek word meaning "the world.") One important reason is a feeling of guilt among Christians. John 17:20-26 is one of the clearest statements on church unity. The writer of this gospel quotes Jesus as saying that those who follow him because of the witness of his disciples "may all be one." The love of the Father for the Son is to be known in the lives of his followers. But does this unity in love mean that all must be in one organization?

The many divisions in Christendom deny the bodily unity that Paul writes about in First Corinthians and Romans 12. Christ is the head. The church is the body, and the different members work together for the common good of the whole body. (*S/R,* 68.) No member is to lord it over another. Each member has the same Spirit. But the history of Christianity has been marked with discord and strife.

As observed in Chapter 7 of this book, in the very earliest days of the church, Christians fell short of the unity they were apparently expected to have in Christ. The early bishops of Rome, Constantinople, Antioch, and Alexandria competed with one another for leadership and influence. The Roman Church claimed to be first in rank. The Romans held that Jesus had said Peter was the rock on which the church was to be built (see Matthew 16:18), and Peter had founded the church at Rome. When the Council of Chalcedon (pronounced *KAL-see-don*) in A.D. 451 de-

151

cided that the powerful churches of Rome and Constantinople should be coequal in rights and authority, the bishop of Rome would not hear of it. Rome claimed that it was the representative of Christ on earth and that all churches should take orders from the Roman bishop.

Political and religious bickering followed, lasting for centuries. Finally in A.D. 1054 the Eastern Orthodox and the Roman Church parted company. It was the first major split. Other splits had occurred but none were as large or significant as the Roman Catholic-Orthodox division. (In recent years, better relations have been established as the pope has met with high leaders of the Orthodox Church.)

THE REFORMATION

The division was further increased with the Protestant Reformation and its aftermath. The Protestant principle emphasized the freedom of each man and his responsibility for his own place before God. It was inevitable that, given the differences in men, a multiplication of sects would develop. In America alone, where this difference was greatest, more than 250 (some say over 500) denominations are known. Even though the vast majority of Protestants in America are members of about eighteen churches, these divisions still have fostered a sense of guilt. The feeling is widespread that so many divisions betray the spirit and intention of Christ's teachings. In a spirit of repentance and renewal the ecumenical movement seeks to overcome a situation that Christ never intended.

Ecumenism also has a practical side. Having so many churches competing with one another, sometimes three or four in the same block, when apparently all of them are trying to win men to Christ, is sheer inefficiency. If they pooled their resources, the job could be done with greater dispatch and less energy. (S/R, 69.) The seminaries could have more teachers, less duplication, and smaller overhead cost if they joined ranks. Ministers could be trained at half the present cost. Millions of dollars could be saved annually and devoted to benevolences if organizational waste was eliminated. In business-conscious America this is certainly one of the main drives in ecumenism.

HOW THE MOVEMENT BEGAN

Modern ecumenicity actually began with missionaries in foreign lands. They found it increasingly difficult to explain Methodist, Baptist, Presbyterian, and Lutheran "brands" of Christianity. European historical differences in practice and belief seemed unimportant in India and Zanzibar. Divisions symbolized the broken body of Christ, rather than Christ as head of the church. Competition and duplication of services increased the economic cost of missions and decreased their efficiency. Co-operation appeared to be a necessity. Disunity was a hindrance to the missionaries' proclamation of the gospel. (See again S/R, 45.)

This concern among the missionaries led to the calling of world conferences of Protestants in New York and London in 1854. Other meetings followed, and in 1910 the World Missionary Conference met at Edinburgh. This Edinburgh conference provided the inspiration out of which the ecumenical movement emerged. Almost all of the later ecumenical leaders were at Edinburgh. J. H. Oldham supervised the planning. John R. Mott, a Methodist layman, was chairman of the meetings.

CRITICS OF THE DIVIDED CHURCHES

The growing power of secularism has also contributed to ecumenism. The divisions among Christians have brought ridicule and sarcasm from nonchurchmen. Non-Christians have been quick to point to the inconsistency between divided Christendom and the teachings of Christ. They also point to the contradictory claims to truth. All of them simply could not be true. As long as the churches remained divided and divisive, their witnesses to the gospel tended to cancel one another.

Nietzsche (pronounced *NEE-che*), one of the greatest critics of Christianity, voiced a virulent form of secularism that has acquired many devotees. There is no God, he said. The churches have been serving themselves with their so-called altruistic ethics and final truths. "One should not enter churches in order to find *fresh* air to breathe." * The churches are really "poison brewers" using a disguise. In their own interests the Christians have stifled the will to power which is back of everything. Nietzsche called for the junking of the disguises of love, sacrifice, and humility. These values produce obliging, sickly, mediocre men. The church has preserved what ought to have perished. Away with constraint. Let man be what he was intended to be. Let the strong prevail. Nietzsche called for "hardness, violence, slavery, peril in the street and in the heart, concealment, Stoicism, temptation, and deviltry of every sort." * For the elevation of man "everything evil, frightful, tyrannical, brutal, and snake-like" * serves as well as anything else. It is not hard to see why Hitler considered Nietzsche his spiritual father.

Another quite different form of secularism found expression in America in John Dewey. He has influenced education more than any other man in the twentieth century; his basic views have indirectly touched millions of people. One learns by doing, said Dewey; therefore, let us do away with all the old memorized dogmas and doctrines. We must wipe the slate clean of everything that belief in a supernatural God entails. For Dewey, Christianity had outgrown its usefulness; it was a thing of the past.

Faced with this kind of militant secularism, Christians began to feel that they must close ranks. Not different voices but a united voice appeared necessary. In the presence of a common foe Christians increasingly felt that they must lay aside their hostilities and co-operate. When Christians began to co-operate, they found the added mutual enrichment of fellowship and new ideas. Old historic differences began to seem less important, and ecumenicity took a giant step forward.

■ Using the "Chart of Key Questions" (Resource Packet, item 4) to guide your study, examine the causes of division and the need for unity within the church.

■ Let a group of three persons engage in a discussion about S/R, 69 before the entire class. All three should have read earlier S/R, 68 and 70. These two readings will give clues to questions they might ask. One person may be responsible for directing the discussion. He/she should begin by reading aloud S/R, 69. The impact of the reading would be greater if one member of the group would prepare a simple turnover chart showing the facts and figures so that the class members can have a view of the entire proposal. The last paragraph can provide the outline for building the chart. The other two persons will respond with questions or remarks. Discuss: What specific ministries would be possible if such a plan were used in your community? Which of the proposals are most acceptable? Why? Least acceptable? Why? What kinds of resistance are most likely to appear? What would be your personal response to such a proposal?

INHERENT DANGERS

The very reasons given *for* ecumenism have also aroused fears in many quarters. It is all very well to talk about the members of the body of Christ working together for the common good, but does this mean we have to be in a super-church? Many Christians feel that one superchurch will mean a loss of doctrine and greater inefficiency because of inevitable bureaucracy. Others want to know if unity will mean some form of compulsory uniformity and therefore the loss of the traditional insights of various Christian groups.

Some changes in doctrines cannot be avoided. Synthesis or the combination of parts means compromise. If one church dominates and dictates, the insights of other churches will suffer. If in a radiance of good feeling no one presses doctrine, the least common denominator of belief will result.

This "common denominator" attitude marks the present state of ecumenical achievement. After the forming of the World Council of Churches at Amsterdam in 1948, a doctrinal stagnation settled over the organization. Belief in Jesus Christ as God and Savior was all that was required of members of the World Council. Many realized that this was not enough but that nothing more could be agreed upon. Consequently, a feeling of sadness and uneasy discomfort prevailed in the very midst of what should have been joyous triumph.

Efficiency is laudable, but whether one big church will be more efficient is questionable. Such a church would be so large that a big bureaucracy with its attendant evils would probably result. The big-business model in the name of efficiency does not commend itself to many Christians.

In the background and history of the ecumenical movement, many dangers have been seen. As a result of the writings of Friedrich Schleiermacher (pronounced *SLY-er-MOCK-er*), King Wilhelm III of Germany decided to unite the Calvinists and Lutherans. Schleiermacher found the basis of religion in experience, in the feeling of dependence on God. Religion no longer appeared to be based on a set of revealed doctrines nor on obedience to the will of God as revealed in the Bible. Basically, said Schleiermacher, religion is an inward feeling of dependence on the Absolute. Both belief and conduct flow from this, but religion is not a body of doctrines. King Wilhelm concluded therefore that there was no reason for Calvinists and Lutherans to continue their old, separate ways.

Many Lutherans did not agree. A man by the name of Klaus Harms was one who felt that Lutheran views were still relevant. In 1817, on the three hundredth anniversary of the appearance of Luther's Ninety-five Theses, Harms published ninety-five theses emphasizing Lutheran beliefs.

The dislike of the forced union of Calvinists and Lutherans initiated the division of which the Missouri Synod of Concordia Lutherans in the United States is a part. Their emphasis falls on doctrine, and that is the reason the Missouri Synod Lutherans are not members of the World Council of Churches.

Some eight hundred Christian evangelicals from the United States, Canada, and Continental Europe united in in 1846 to form the Evangelical Alliance in London. The Alliance promoted religious freedom, advocated missions, served as an ecumenical press service, and stimulated a sense of unity among Christians. It was not officially representative of the churches; participation was by individuals.

UNITY WITHOUT DOCTRINE

Large groups of Christians have proceeded to find a way of co-operating without doctrinal agreement. They have deemed fellowship and a common voice on social issues sufficient fruit from their loose unity. Doctrines can wait or may not even be necessary. (*S/R,* 70.)

On this basis the Federal Council of the Churches of Christ in America was organized in 1908. It was a federation only, "with no authority to draw upon a common creed or form of government or of worship or in any way to limit the full autonomy of the Christian bodies adhering to it." It sought only to discuss and to give advice. In 1950 when it merged with other interdenominational agencies to form the National Council of the Churches of Christ in the United States of America, it represented churches with a total membership of 32 million individuals.

The National Council of Churches is not a superchurch as some people seem to think. It has, however, become the conscience of Protestantism on many living issues. It aims to plainly show the essential oneness of Christian churches in Jesus Christ, to express fellowship, and to try to apply the law of Christ to every aspect of human living. From the beginning its strong social emphasis has made it unpopular with many conservatives. (*S/R,* 71.) Nevertheless, the National Council of Churches continues to grow and to perform vital roles for the churches. Similar organizations have blossomed in France, Switzerland, Germany, New Zealand, Australia, Great Britain, and Canada. They indicate how far unity can go without doctrinal agreement.

In the fervor of unity, churches with common family backgrounds began to unite early in the twentieth century, so that this century is properly called the century of ecumenism. Healing the visible disunity appeared to be paramount. The Methodists overcame their Civil War animosities and formed The Methodist Church in 1939. As has already been mentioned, the Evangelical Church and the Church of the United Brethren in Christ united in 1946 to become The Evangelical United Brethren Church. Now the latter has joined with The Methodist Church to become The United Methodist Church.

These mergers, however, were not unanimous. Some groups bitterly opposed them and remained outside. But the trend in this century has been and still is toward greater organic union, especially on the national level among churches with similar histories.

■ How may Christian churches achieve a unity in fellowship and action if not in doctrine? Consider some specific cases. Work in groups of six to eight persons. Let each group consider how churches might act in *one* of the following situations:

    A. A section of your town is slated for urban renewal.

    B. In the high school, it has been discovered that 20 per cent of the senior girls drop out because of pregnancy.

    C. It has been discovered that one fourth of the annual budget of the local government has been spent for various kinds of graft and bribery.

    D. In the community 25 per cent of the young men examined for induction into the armed services are rejected for mental and physical reasons.

Use some of these questions to guide your work: How could churches work together in dealing with such problems? Why should there be joint efforts? What would be the advantages here of being united in one church? How might differences in denominations be advantageous? Is working together worth the compromises on doctrine? Is unity worth the inevitable bureaucracy?

THE WORLD COUNCIL OF CHURCHES

Early in the twenties the enthusiasm for ecumenical co-operation was strong. The major Protestant churches put aside their traditional differences on the Lord's Supper, ordination, church government, and held a Conference on *Life and Work* at Stockholm in 1925. They felt that the importance of the world's social ills was so great that action had to take priority over doctrine.

Other churchmen, however, had begun to believe that co-operation without a doctrinal basis left the whole ecumenical movement a prey to shallow optimism. Consequently, in 1927 under the inspiration of Charles H. Brent, an American Episcopal missionary bishop, the *Faith and Order* Conference met at Lausanne, Switzerland. There representatives of world Protestantism frankly faced the doctrinal differences that separated them, particularly the doctrines of the ministry and the sacraments.

In 1937 these two movements toward ecumenism voted to join their efforts and to establish a World Council of Churches. The Second World War delayed the official formation of the World Council until 1948. There delegates from 144 church groups, representing 44 countries, participated in organizing the World Council. While acceptance of Jesus Christ as God and Savior was the only belief required of members, doctrines have since received increasing attention. The New Delhi meeting in 1961 linked the doctrine of Jesus Christ as the light of the world with a strong appeal to all world governments to eliminate war, to stop rattling bombs, to substitute reason for force, to strengthen the United Nations, and to enhance the dignity of man.

Throughout the ecumenical movement in the twentieth century the inherent danger of fellowship without doctrinal unity looms. The International Council of Christian Churches, a fundamentalistic organization which actively opposes the World Council of Churches, is a continual reminder that the divisive breaches in Christendom have not been overcome. Barriers blocking a superchurch are still formidable.

■ How important is a doctrinal basis for unity among churches? Here again, *S/R*, 68 and 70 are appropriate. Consider the fact that both the Confession of Faith of the EUB's and the Methodist Articles of Religion appear in the new *Discipline* of The United Methodist Church. One person might obtain copies of these to read aloud. Your minister may help you locate them. Do you consider it necessary that both be printed? Why? What is the effect on unity attempts when persons react to the *wording* of doctrinal statements? To what degree do people defend a view because it has been traditionally accepted? How are the underlying attitudes in this discussion related to unity?

■ Study the pictures after *S/R*, 44 in the book of selected readings entitled *We Have This Heritage*. How important is it to us to be able to meet the world's needs, if the task can be accomplished only by co-operating with other denominations?

Listen as one person reads aloud Matthew 28:19-20. Another may read again John 17. In what ways do the activities in the pictures fulfill Christ's prayer and Christ's command, and how do they fall short of fulfillment? How central to the nature and mission of the church is the type of ministry being pictured?

THE ROMAN CATHOLIC STANCE

In previous chapters, we have discussed the attitude of the Roman Catholic Church toward change. Does this mean Catholics are drawing further away from Protestants?

Vatican Council II has radically altered the Roman Catholic attitude toward unity. (*S/R*, 72.) Co-operation between Catholics and non-Catholics has become the order of the day. Priests in America now feel free to associate with Protestants. They can worship and pray with them. Protestant hymns can be heard in Catholic churches. They are using the Revised Standard Version Bible; a joint committee of Protestant and Catholic scholars have begun a new translation of the Bible. In a few instances (though without papal approval) Catholics have taken communion with Protestants.

Roman Catholics are enrolling in Protestant divinity schools in increasing numbers in this country. Such enrollment now exceeds two hundred. Some young priests are taking their clinical training in Protestant churches. More and more Roman Catholic teachers are appearing on the faculties of Protestant seminaries and vice versa. Many Protestant-Catholic schools are offering joint courses in ecumenism, and some have worked out professorial exchanges. A Missouri Synod Lutheran minister joined the department of sociology at Loyola University in 1966, and a member of the Church of Christ became president of the Sacred Heart Dominican College for Women in Houston.

Such interchanges simply were not possible a few years ago. Today they are not isolated examples of ecumenism. They can be duplicated in many communities. Many observers believe that a new and *irreversible* trend has really begun in Catholicism. Pope Paul VI has even implied that the belief in papal infallibility may be changed. It certainly must be faced as the greatest single barrier to ecumenicity with Protestants now. But ecumenism moves slowly, and few have dared to hope that real unity will emerge in this century. After all, Protestants have not yet united.

Until the time of Pope John XXIII, the Roman Catholic Church remained adamantly opposed to a council of churches, saying there can be only one church, the Roman Church. Ecumenism to Catholics before Pope John meant that those who had separated from Rome should return to the fold. Rome refused to participate in ecumenical discussions on the ground that its truth might thereby be tainted. A papal letter in 1928 bluntly stated, "There is but one way in which the unity of Christians may be fostered, and that is by furthering the return to the one true Church of Christ of those who are separated from it." Those in error must "submit"

161

themselves fully to Rome's teaching and government. Roman Catholics were warned to shun Protestant ecumenical undertakings.

This stance was slightly modified in 1943 by a pronouncement that allowed Catholic scholars to exchange views with other scholars on the Bible. In 1949 selected and trained Catholic leaders were allowed to explain the Catholic faith to non-Catholic groups. Such leaders were forbidden to gloss over differences and were warned that talks with non-Catholics were "in fact a source of danger only to be permitted after most careful investigation." When the Catholic Church in 1950 proclaimed as essential belief that the Virgin Mary had been taken bodily up into heaven, the door to ecumenical co-operation seemed to be closing.

Then in 1962 the sessions of Vatican II opened. The change in Catholicism was immediately noticeable. Rome royally treated Protestant observers, even invited their opinions on many issues. *The Documents of Vatican II*, edited by W. M. Abbott, S.J., included Protestant responses to the papal pronouncements. All over the world, liberal Roman Catholics are speaking bluntly about one church, not necessarily the Roman Catholic Church. An openness has been born in Roman Catholicism that seeks not to pontificate and tyrannize but to listen and learn. Pope Paul VI demonstrated this openness in his trip to Turkey in July, 1967, when he met Orthodox Patriarch Athenagoras and increased hopes of bringing closer together the two branches of Christendom which split in 1054.

With the wide-ranging talks about union among Protestants, with the unusual freedom in Roman Catholicism, a new era appears to be dawning in ecumenism. Unity in diversity is no longer a dream, and one organic Christian church is now seen by some people as a possibility. Historical diversity continues and will undoubtedly do so for a long time to come, but significant strides toward unity in the body of Christ have been made. Men have begun to think that in God's providence the search for unity may not be endless.

The words with which Vatican II opened in 1962 may be prophetic: "At this moment of history, Providence is leading us toward a new order of human relations which, by the work of men and for the most part beyond their expectations, are developing towards the fulfillment of higher and unforeseen designs."

■ Plan as a class to attend a Roman Catholic Mass. If possible, have the priest explain the Mass to your class before you attend. Also, ask the priest to plan a discussion period following the Mass when you might talk with him and an informed Roman Catholic layman. You might discuss issues such as: the current dissent among Roman Catholics about celibacy of priests and liturgical reform. Discuss together the meaning of Vatican II for local Christian cooperation and for Protestant-Catholic relationships. A committee from the class might investigate recent books or news articles about Vatican II to help them plan specific questions to have the priest discuss.

■ If you cannot attend a Mass, let each person list on paper the questions that have come to mind as he or she has read or heard about Vatican II. Let a committee use the questions to interview a priest, then report back to the group.

■ Close the session by reading aloud in unison stanzas 1 and 2 of "Eternal God, Whose Power Upholds" (*The Methodist Hymnal*, 476).

■ Let the leadership team be prepared to give assignments for the next chapter of study and the members of the group be prepared to accept the assignments.

NOTES ON CHAPTER 10

Page 149: Quoted in Edgar Dewitt Jones, *Lincoln and the Preachers* (Harper and Row, 1948), page 141.

Page 154: Friedrich Nietzsche, *Beyond Good and Evil* (Henry Regnery Company, 1955), page 36. Used by permission.

Page 154: *Beyond Good and Evil*, page 50. Used by permission.

Page 154: *Beyond Good and Evil*, page 50. Used by permission.

Read these selections in your Bible:
Micah 6:1-8
What the Lord requires.

Matthew 5:43-48
The command to be perfect.

Romans 8:1-17
Free from the law of sin and death.

11

□□

SHOULD METHODISM DIE?

Who are Methodists? How did Methodism begin? How did we become what we are? What do we believe? What is our basic authority? What is distinctive about Methodism? How do we stand on social issues? What attitudes do we take toward learning? Will the movement toward church unity mean the end of Methodism?

These and similar questions are often heard in Methodist circles. Answers to them should reveal something about our heritage and help us to understand what we are now.

WHO ARE WE?

"A Methodist," said John Wesley, "is one who has the love of God shed abroad in his heart by the Holy Ghost given unto him, one who loves the Lord his God with all his heart, with all his soul, with all his mind, and with all his

---

■ *As you arrive at your place of meeting, check the assignment chart for specific preparation to be made before the session begins.*
■ *Set goals for your study of this chapter as suggested on page 15.*

strength." That is all very good, but it tells us little about Methodists.

Methodism did not begin as a new sect in Christianity; it began as a religious movement within the Church of England. (The Church of England is sometimes called the Anglican Church.) If Wesley's wishes had prevailed, it would have remained in the Anglican fold; there would have been no separate Methodist church. But history did not work out that way.

Methodism had its beginning in the vow of John Wesley in 1725 "to set in earnest upon a new life." After being ordained as a minister in the Church of England in 1728, he returned to Oxford University, where he had studied earlier.

Soon he became the leader of a small group of students seriously seeking righteousness, the Holy Club. Because they strictly scheduled every hour of the day, they were laughed at and called "Methodists." For taking the Lord's Supper every week and studiously examining their lives, they were called "Sacramentarians." For their regular reading of the New Testament in Greek, they were called "Bible Moths." They met every night in Wesley's or another's room, fasted on Wednesday and Fridays, and visited the sick, the poor, and prisoners in jail. They attended regular public worship and out of their limited funds supported charity schools.

In reading the Bible they found inward and outward holiness which they strove to show in their lives. George Whitefield, a member of the Holy Club, commented, "And never did persons, I believe, strive more earnestly to enter in at the straight gate. They kept their bodies under even to an extreme. They were dead to the world . . . so that they might win Christ. Their hearts glowed with the love of God." *

During this period, as Wesley clearly says in his *Journal,* he was trying desperately to earn his way to heaven. In 1735, Wesley came to the American Colonies as a missionary in Georgia. Later he said he came to save his own soul. Early in 1738, he returned to England, a failure as a missionary and with no certainty of his own salvation. In a prayer meeting in London on May 24, 1738, he gained that inward assurance. He learned that the key to reconciliation with God is not the feverish keeping of rules or the doing of good deeds but in trust in God. (*S/R*, 73.)

Wesley organized small societies, like the one at Oxford, for those who wanted to seek righteousness more earnestly than the usual ways the Anglican Church afforded. This was not a substitute for faith; it was an attempt to live disciplined new life in faith. In 1743 Wesley adopted rules for his united societies which are still printed in *Doctrines and Discipline of the Methodist Church*. To enter a society, one needed only "a desire to flee from the wrath to come, to be saved from his sins." To stay, he had to conform to the rules.

Wesley regarded his new societies as organizations within the Church of England, not as new churches. His traveling preachers were not ordained. They were to take communion in the Anglican Church. To the Anglicans, who had had so much trouble in the previous century, Wesley's societies looked like dissenting splinter groups. He found himself and his societies increasingly shut out of the churches, but his followers multiplied by the thousands. They acquired property and preaching places. In 1744 they held their first conference, a "Conversation," to discuss freely every problem of doctrine, discipline, and education. Wesley did not approve of the term *Methodist Church*, but it was used as early as 1759 by his co-workers, John Fletcher and Vincent Perronet.

By the time of Wesley's death in 1791, Methodists in England numbered more than 135,000. Many of these regarded themselves as Anglicans, but for all practical purposes the Methodists were a separate people. In 1795 the Methodists voted to let each society decide whether its preachers should administer sacraments. This was practical separation, even though some societies forbade their preachers to administer the sacraments for another century. Gradually the Methodists undertook to ordain "ministers." Thus the Methodists *emerged* out of the Church of England.

AMERICAN METHODISM

Seven years before Wesley's death in 1791, American Methodists formally broke with Anglicanism and established The Methodist Episcopal Church. Frontier conditions and the Revolutionary War were the chief causes. By 1773 the Methodists in America numbered 1,160. Technically they were members of the Church of England in America.

In 1784, Wesley decided to ordain in England a "superintendent" who would have power to ordain men in America. Wesley then "set apart" Thomas Coke as the superintendent of the American societies, a position which Wesley wrote he was to share with Francis Asbury. Francis Asbury was born in England, but he came to the Colonies in 1771. (*S/R*, 74.)

At the "Christmas Conference" in Baltimore, Maryland, in December, 1784, the Methodist ministers in America constituted themselves The Methodist Episcopal Church and Coke and Asbury were made superintendents. Philip Otterbein, a German minister and later cofounder of the United Brethren Church, assisted in the consecration of Asbury.

The Christmas Conference adopted a form of Discipline modeled after Wesley's suggestions, voted to have twenty-five Articles of Religion dealing with Christian beliefs, accepted the form of worship suggested by Wesley, passed a rule against ministers' drinking intoxicating liquors, planned to "extirpate the abomination of slavery," and decided to found a college.

■ Let a member of the leadership team prepare on newsprint or chalkboard a list of the main points of the General Rules in the *Discipline.*

On the basis of these disciplinary rules, discuss these questions: What are some ways for accomplishing what Wesley wanted to accomplish through these rules? Knowing that we do not keep all of these rules, how can we determine necessary elements of a new

167

form of discipline? Should we as Methodists observe *any* rules? If so what should they be? (As members of the class suggest rules, have one person list these on newsprint or chalkboard.)

Compare your rules with Wesley's. Why do you consider yours better? At what points are they inferior to Wesley's rules?

■ Let one person summarize the reasons John Wesley began his societies. This information is in the preceding pages of this text.

Now, use the circular response method (each person in turn is asked to respond) for considering these questions: What are the driving forces that cause you to continue going through the "accepted religious motions"? Why is it important for you to be an active member of the church?

WHAT DO WE BELIEVE?

History helps us to see how we started, but what do we believe? What is our basic authority? Do we believe in the Bible? Do we believe in the Virgin Birth, heaven and hell, a creed, birth control, social action?

No one should presume to speak for all Methodists, but traditional lines of belief are clearly discernible. Wesley himself was all his life a minister of the Church of England. He accepted the Thirty-nine Articles of belief of the Church of England. But Methodism began as an organized revival movement with pietistic leanings. (See Chaper 8 and *S/ R,* 53 and 54.) It asserted its own distinctive character, influenced by the early church fathers, Luther, Calvin, and the Moravians.

Calvinism was strong in Wesley's thought, but he was never able to accept election of some to salvation and of others to damnation. The issue caused him to part company with George Whitefield in 1741 just after Wesley published his sermon on "Free Grace." Wesley fervently believed that salvation was possible for *all:* "The grace or love of God, whence cometh our salvation, is free in all, and free for all. . . . Christ died for the ungodly!" This belief stood at the very heart of the Methodist movement and echoed in many of Charles Wesley's hymns.

In spite of his debt to the Moravians, Wesley parted company with them over their belief that to be saved one had to refrain from doing anything. One could not read the Bible, take communion, or even pray, for if he did (some Moravians believed) he might think his salvation was in some way from himself rather than totally from God. Therefore, one must wait for mystical assurance of absolute salvation.

Wesley was unwilling to wait. His heart had been strangely warmed at Aldersgate Street; the fruits of his preaching convinced him that his faith was accompanied by the power of the Spirit. That was assurance enough; assurance of absolute salvation he never had. Doubts assailed him, even late in life. (S/R, 75.)

Wesley's conviction that every Christian should grow in holiness, that he should actively show the fruits of faith in good works, brought forth the charge of Arminianism. Emphasis on the rules of the societies seemed to reinforce this notion. Wesley believed emphatically in disciplined Christian living but he did not believe man can merit salvation. Accept the gift offered in Christ, yes; merit the gift, no.

According to the twenty-five Articles of Religion, Methodists believe in the Trinity, the divine-human nature of Christ, the Resurrection, the sufficiency of the Scriptures for salvation, original or birth sin, free will, justification by faith, good works, forgiveness for those who truly repent, two sacraments—Baptism and the Lord's Supper, participation in government, and heaven and hell. According to the same articles, Methodists do not believe in purgatory, works of supererogation, prayer to saints, conducting worship in a tongue not understood by the people, enforced celibacy for ministers, transubstantiation, withholding the cup from the laity, a communism of goods, or uniform ceremonies and rites.

Explanations of what these mean would vary widely, depending on education and other factors. Some Methodists picture heaven with mansions and streets of gold and hell with roaring furnaces. Others might say hell is the absence of the Spirit of Christ; heaven is its presence. Some believe the Virgin Birth literally. Others believe it as a theological expression of Christ's divinity. In Methodism wide variations of fundamentalism and liberalism exist side by side. This fact indicates that fellowship is more important than subscription to a creed. Despite some heresy trials, tolerance and freedom of expression are marks of Methodism. This is so much the case that some people seeing so many diverse views wonder if the Methodists believe anything. (S/R, 76.)

Such variation is possible because there is no final authority in Methodism beyond the minimum of beliefs found in the baptismal vows. There is no pope, no creed required for every Methodist. Bishops are not infallible. General traditions provide guidelines rather than requirements, thus placing responsibility for decisions squarely on the individual.

The Bible and the "cumulative witness of Christian experience" are the closest things to authority in Methodism. According to the Articles of Religion, "The Holy Scriptures contain all things necessary to salvation; so that whatsoever is not read therein, nor may be proved thereby, is not to be required of any man that it should be believed as an article of faith, or be thought requisite or necessary to salvation." * But nothing is said about how the Bible is to be interpreted! Wesley himself turned to other persons and writings to help him in his search for salvation. He said in the "Preface to His Sermons" that on spiritual questions he sought help from the Bible first. Then,

> if any doubt still remains, I consult those who are experienced in the things of God; and then the writings whereby, being dead, they yet speak. And what I thus learn, that I teach.*

Episcopal and conference pronouncements usually have influence in Methodist circles; but this influence is the force of moral persuasion. It is not binding law. Freedom versus discipline poses problems in modern Methodism. Each has advantages and disadvantages. Historically, trials of erring members are no longer held. A shapeless tolerance prevails. This apathy (the attitude is probably more nearly one of apathy than toleration, if we are honest) is one of the greatest departures from Wesley. While Wesley said, "Think and let think," he nevertheless strictly enforced the rules of his societies. Today organizational rules prevail more strongly than articles of belief.

■ Understanding Methodism necessarily involves some knowledge of traditional beliefs. See *S/R*, 76. Use the "Chart of Key Questions" (Resource Packet, item 4) to help you examine the major beliefs. Specific suggestions are included in the Leaders' Guide in the packet.

In connection with the study of the chart read *S/R*, 56. How do you feel about Wesley's tolerance of other points of view? If each person is entitled to his own interpretation, why is the search for theological truth necessary or important?

SOCIAL ACTION

While Wesley is not known as a social reformer, his preaching generated a sense of social responsibility. His goal was victory over sin in individual and social relationships. He believed that by planting the ideal of holiness in the hearts of men both church and nation would undergo reform. In this respect Wesley was a product of the Reformation. Following the warnings of Matthew 25 he visited the prisons to relieve the physical as well as the spiritual needs of the prisoners, yet he made no attempt to change the system. He furiously opposed slavery, one of the greatest social blights of the time. In his last letter he urged William Wilberforce to fight slavery: "Go in the name of God and in the power of His might, till even American Slavery, the vilest that ever saw the sun, shall vanish away before it." * Methodists provided strong support for Wilberforce in his struggle to abolish slavery in the nineteenth century.

Wesley spoke out against smuggling, political dishonesty, drunkenness, and indolence. He urged the prohibition of distilling so that the grain might be used to feed the hungry.

He did not believe that the poor are under the judgment of God, nor did he believe their plight was the result of idleness. He helped them with medicines, loans, and educational pamphlets, convinced that social conditions would change as a consequence of individual conversions. (S/R, 77.)

Methodists in America early expressed concern for social ills, particularly slavery which the conferences of 1780 and 1784 condemned as an abomination to be totally destroyed as soon as possible. The Christmas Conference of 1784 called for the exclusion of any Methodists who did not make provisions within a year to emancipate their slaves. However, those living in states in which emancipation was unlawful were exempted.

In some respects the American Methodists as a result of the War for Independence possessed a greater sense of freedom than their English brethren. The appreciation for freedom enabled them to form a new church. It accounts in large measure for a line of freedom running through American Methodism causing it to split into separate groups in 1845 over the slavery issue. Circuit riders on the frontier soon dropped the formal services recommended by Wesley.

In other respects an individualistic piety prevailed. The image of Methodists that one encounters today, and not without historical reason, is that of legalists who neither smoke nor drink. This was in keeping with the nineteenth century's emphasis on individual morals rather than broad social concerns. The line separating the saved and the unsaved was frequently the line separating those who did not drink whiskey, roll dice, play poker, smoke, dance, swear, fight, and go to the theater and those who did. (S/R, 78.)

The Episcopal Address in the General Conference in 1884 spoke of legal prohibition of liquor as "the platform on which we stand as a denomination, and upon which we will battle until Constitutional Prohibition is secured in every State and Territory in the Union, and finally embodied in the Constitution of the United States." * Methodists supported the Prohibition Party at the turn of the century and a variety of temperance movements. Eventually prohibition became an amendment to the Constitution (1920) only to be repealed in 1933.

Goaded by the rise of the social gospel, the 1908 General Conference of the Methodist Episcopal Church devoted much of its time to social problems and adopted the famous "Methodist Social Creed." The text is worth quoting for it marks a trend away from pietistic individualism:

The Methodist Episcopal Church stands—

For equal rights and complete justice for all men in all stations of life.

For the principle of conciliation and arbitration in industrial dissensions.

For the protection of the worker from dangerous machinery, occupational diseases, injuries, and mortality.

For the abolition of child labor.

For such regulation of the conditions of labor for women as shall safeguard the physical and moral health of the community.

For the suppression of the "sweating system."

For the gradual and reasonable reduction of the hours of labor to the lowest practical point, with work for all; and for that degree of leisure for all which is the condition of the highest human life.

For a release from employment one day in seven.

For a living wage in every industry.

For the highest wage that each industry can afford, and for the most equitable division of the products of industry that can ultimately be devised.

For the recognition of the Golden Rule and the mind of Christ as the supreme law of society and the sure remedy for all social ills.

What do Methodists believe about social action today? No one answer can be given, but the 1964 edition of *Doctrines and Discipline of The Methodist Church*, paragraph 1820,

173

asserts that Methodists "have an obligation to affirm our position on social and economic questions. . . . Jesus taught us to love our neighbors and seek justice for them as well as for ourselves. To be silent in the face of need, injustice, and exploitation is to deny him." The paragraph further states that all men are brothers, equal in the eyes of God, the Father of all peoples, that Jesus died for the redemption of all men, and that we "should live to help save man from sin and from every influence which would harm or destroy him."

The creed then applies this theological basis to the family, the economic order, responsible use of power, poverty and unemployment, wealth, working conditions, social benefits for workers, collective bargaining, Christian vocation, alcohol problems, crime and rehabilitation, gambling, mental health and medical care, drug abuse, sex, social welfare, human rights, civil liberties, world peace, and military service.

■ Review the section of this chapter entitled "Social Action." Pay particular attention to the text of the Social Creed on page 173 and in *Doctrines and Discipline of The Methodist Church* (1964), paragraph 1820.

Discuss: In what ways are your standards of value and your ways of acting compatible with the principles embodied in the Social Creed?

Divide the class into four groups. Each group will study a teaching picture (Resource Packet, items 1A, 1B, 1C, and 1D). Consult the Leaders' Guide in the packet for specific instructions. If the class is quite large these four groups may break into pairs or groups of four to six persons to work after viewing the pictures.

Discuss: Based on the answers given to the question about the relation of the Social Creed to the thoughts and actions of the class members, what are your feelings about what the picture shows?

Let each group select one person to use the picture during the week to get reactions of persons not connected with the church. Each group might prepare questions about the picture for the interviewer to use. In the next session hear the reports of the interviewers.

PIETY AND LEARNING

Can educational institutions today be trusted to build up rather than destroy faith? This question is frequently asked by Methodists. It points to a distrust of learning which still lingers in Methodism. (*S/R*, 79.)

Because Wesley regarded himself as an Anglican, and the Anglicans had good schools, Wesley did not greatly concern himself with education. Of his charity schools only the one at Kingswood is worth mentioning. He established it in 1739 for the education of coal miners' children. In 1748 it was enlarged to train children "in every branch of useful learning."

Since Wesley used itinerant preachers who had little education, a practice scorned by the Anglicans, some persons have concluded that Wesley was not interested in education. Although he himself was highly educated, he did object to the stifling of the Spirit that much of the education of the day produced. A warm heart, fervent singing, stirring sermons, and earnestness in prayer seemed more important than cultivated reason that might lead a man away from Scripture and into pride. Wesley strongly rebuked Coke and Asbury for founding a college and naming it Cokesbury after themselves:

> But in one point, my dear brother, I am a little afraid both the Doctor and you differ from me. I study to be little: you study to be great. I creep: you strut along. I found a school: you a college! Nay, and call it after your own names! O beware, do not seek to be something! Let me be nothing, and "Christ be all in all!" *

In America the Christmas Conference of 1784 authorized a college, largely at the insistence of Coke. Asbury wanted to settle for a school, seeing little need for higher education for his frontier-riding preachers. Within ten days over 1,000 pounds (the English money system was used in the colonies at the time) had been subscribed for the new college. Before the year 1785 ended Cokesbury College was established at Abingdon, Maryland. Ten years later it burned. Asbury wrote to a friend, "I wished and prayed that if it was not for his glory it might be destroyed." The college had made great

175

inroads on his time and energy. Nevertheless, in 1797 a successor was built at Baltimore. When it, too, burned to the ground before the year was out, both Asbury and Coke were convinced that God did not want a college for Methodists.

The Methodist contribution to education has been incalculable. The pioneers pushed aside obscurantism and effectively joined piety and learning; they helped make education democratic. "Christian education has its roots in the nature of the Christian gospel itself. Jesus is frequently called Master or Teacher, and he is the authority in our church's program of Christian nurture." * If indeed our colleges and seminaries cannot be trusted, we must still run the risk, for we cannot turn back the clock to an uneducated ministry.

■ Have a panel of four persons (one person will act as moderator) discuss these questions: How has the church benefited from the research and activity of the various disciplines: theology, archeology, sociology, psychology, natural sciences? How can/do persons justify a distrust of education when related to "religious" matters but support it enthusiastically when related to all other "realms" of life? How can they encourage increasing education for professional leaders in every other field but distrust it for professional religious leaders? What attitudes underlying S/R, 79 still influence our thinking? How may/does knowledge cause a loss of a certain kind of faith for some persons? When might such a loss be good? How may increasing knowledge contribute to growing faith? If education is dangerous to ministers, why has the church been traditionally concerned to establish colleges for laymen? How necessary is the Christian college for the future?

SCHISM AND ECUMENISM

The first split in Methodism occurred at the First General Conference in 1792 at Baltimore. James O'Kelley of Virginia resented the life election and the authority of bishops. After several days of debate, he and others withdrew to form the Republican Methodists. Many of them later merged with Barton W. Stone and the Campbells to form the Disciples of Christ. Basically the same problem of more democratic leadership in the church caused the formation of the Methodist Protestant Church in 1830. To a less important degree, it also figured in the formation of the Wesleyan Methodist Church in 1843 which had lay representation and no bishops.

The great schism came in 1844 when the Methodist Episcopal Church split over the question of slavery. The following year the Methodist Episcopal Church, South was organized. The first general conference of the southern church was held in 1846. Negro dissatisfaction with treatment received in white churches caused the formation of the African Methodist Episcopal Church in 1816 and the African Methodist Episcopal Zion Church in 1820.

Feeling that Wesley's doctrine of perfection had been neglected, the Free Methodist Church was organized in 1860. For the remainder of the century the question of holiness rocked the churches. At least ten groups with Methodist backgrounds formed in the last six years of the century, the nucleus being the First Church of the Nazarene, in Los Angeles, California.

The twentieth century has been a different story. In 1939 the Methodist Protestant Church, the Methodist Episcopal Church, South, and the Methodist Episcopal Church put aside their differences to unite as The Methodist Church.

The union between The Methodist Church and The Evangelical United Brethren Church as The United Methodist Church is now accomplished. Both churches have a common evangelical heritage in the early history of the United States with roots reaching back to the Reformation.

To return to the question asked in the title of this chapter: Should Methodism die? There are some who feel that eventually all denominations should be dissolved into one great church made up of all Christians. We have seen, however, that many factors lie behind the origins and continuation of denominations and sects. Doubtless, these factors would continue to operate, so that new churches might arise faster than unions would occur.

177

At the present time, any union involving The United Methodist Church is quite distant. If proposals are made that would respect the distinctive Wesleyan tradition *within* a larger church, Methodists will face a difficult decision on what God's will might be.

■ Close the session by reading responsively, John 17.

■ Let the leadership team be prepared to give assignments for the next chapter of study and the members of the group be prepared to accept the assignments.

NOTES ON CHAPTER 11

Page 165: Quoted in Francis H. Tees, *Methodist Origins* (Parthenon Press, 1948), page 15. Copyright 1948 by Francis H. Tees.

Page 170: *Doctrines and Discipline of The Methodist Church*, paragraph 65.

Page 170: Quoted in *Wesley's Standard Sermons*, edited by E. H. Sugden (Epworth Press, 1955), volume 1, page 32. Used by permission.

Page 171: Quoted in Maldwyn L. Edwards, *John Wesley and the Eighteenth Century* (Epworth Press, 1955), page 123.

Page 172: *Journal of the General Conference, 1884*, pages 238-39 and Appendix, page 392.

Page 175: Quoted in *The Letters of John Wesley*, edited by John Telford (Epworth Press, 1931), volume 8, page 91.

Page 176: *Doctrines and Discipline of The Methodist Church*, paragraph 1324.

Read these selections in your Bible:
Job 19:1-12
How long will you torment me?

Psalms 80:1-19
Restore us, O Lord.

Revelation 21:1-8
A new heaven and a new earth.

12

□□

WHERE DO THE SIGNS POINT?

At few times in the past have Christians asked as many questions as they are asking today. People are anxious about the future of the church. Is the gospel still relevant? Will the church continue as an important institution in our society? Will Christian attitudes continue to inform the conscience of Western man? Can the drives toward ecumenicity be sustained? Is the social revolution more than the church can cope with?

The 1960's have witnessed an extraordinary revival of interest in theology. People are concerned. They are concerned about race relations, the war in Vietnam, poverty, urban renewal, the inner city, mental health, senior citizens, anti-Christian attitudes, ethics, personal integrity, sex, suffering,

---

■ *As you arrive at your place of meeting, check the assignment chart for specific preparation to be made before the session begins.*
■ *Set goals for your study of this chapter as suggested on page 15.*

179

and death. They have not found the voice of the churches terribly exciting or relevant to these concerns. (S/R, 80.) In most churches membership has been increasing. The *Yearbook of American Churches,* including Jewish congregations, showed 49 per cent of our population held church membership in 1940. In 1950, 57 per cent belonged to churches, and in 1960 the figures leaped to 63.6 per cent. There the figures began topping out. But increasing membership does not mean increasing influence. (S/R, 81.)

The specter of decline of influence has caused churchmen to ask why this happened and what can be done about it. Theological schools are revamping their curricula and methods. Many churches have developed new programs and have updated old ones to meet specific needs. Ecclesiastical flexibility has often been impressive, but just as often repressive. One of the major divisions in Christendom, potentially as divisive as the Reformation cleavage, is between churchmen who favor change and those who do not.

The contemporary church in America is torn by tensions. It is rocked by forces that it cannot control and does not understand. The relevance of the Christian experience is not clear even to church members. On the one hand, critics demand that the church provide moral leadership in the struggle for justice and peace, but agreement on how this should be done is lacking. Other critics demand that the church attend to its spiritual tasks and stay out of peace demonstrations, the fight for civil rights, and political hassles. (S/R, 82.) Local congregations often lag behind their ministers on the social issues of the day at a time when laymen are supposed to be recognizing their role as the church. National bodies and conventions, composed largely of the clergy, denounced segregation long before local congregations bestirred themselves. Ministers march in demonstrations in greater proportionate numbers than their constituents. Cartoons have begun to appear about ministers off demonstrating

while their flocks are unattended. The laity often seems re-
luctant to follow the advice and example of the clergy.

■ Begin this session by hearing the reports of the persons who
were to ask unchurched persons to react to the pictures that were
used in the last session. (See page 174.) Discuss: How do their
reactions compare with those expressed in your groups?

■ Is religion influencing life today? After reading pages 179-81 of
this chapter and S/R, 81, let three persons have a discussion before
the entire class. Each one should express his reasons for agreeing or
disagreeing with the three conclusions drawn in the selected reading.
Then let the whole class respond to this question: What, in your
opinion, is each of the conclusions *really* saying? Do you agree or
disagree? Why?

■ Use the "Chart of Key Questions" (Resource Packet, item 4) to
guide your study of the main issues in this chapter. Detailed directions are included in the Leaders' Guide in the packet. This will
complete your work with the chart. The leadership team, or a
committee assigned in advance, might be prepared to use the chart
at the conclusion of this session to review and summarize the unit.

THE STATE OF AMERICAN CHRISTIANITY

A relationship can be seen between four contemporary
literary trends and various perspectives on the state of American Christianity today.

The first is that of disillusionment, of a nauseous feeling
that life is absurd and God is far away. Existence is barren,
a hell from which there is no escape. The dramatist, Samuel
Beckett, exemplifies this trend. In his play, *Waiting for
Godot,* he pictures two quietly desperate men as they wait
for Godot (a substitute word for God), who never arrives.
Their attempted suicide is unsuccessful, so they have nothing
to do but to come back tomorrow and continue the absurd
process of waiting.

Some say that the church is an outdated defense of a past
culture, that its life is meaningless, and that its members
perpetuate senseless forms because they cannot turn else-
where. They wait for God, but he is absent—and he will not
come.

181

A second literary trend is that which presents the Christian life as the answer to life's most pressing problems. Graham Greene puts forth this point of view: God is present in his children, who discern and do his will. In *The Power and the Glory,* he depicts a Roman Catholic priest in Mexico that is torn by a revolution. This priest, fleeing the authorities and searching for a new inspiration, leads his mule through the jungle and contemplates what God is like. He remembers how he had responded to questions about what God was like when he had instructed children who were preparing to join the church. He had told them that God, in his great love for them, was like their father or mother. He had also likened the love of God to the close relationships the children had shared with other members of their families. Yet now he feels that beneath this somewhat simple answer there is a great mystery. God is not only parent but also policeman, criminal, and judge.

Thus, the priest identifies man with the image of God; man cannot be understood apart from his relationship with his Creator. There are those who feel that the church is fulfilling its mission when its members identify themselves with those pathetic souls who are discriminated against and deprived of the basic rights of human dignity. In the spirit of Christ, they minister unto those for whom he died.

The third trend is that in which the authors drift away from a purely Christian focus and attempt to find purpose outside the monolithic, institutionalized church. Such an author is a Frenchman, Georges Bernanos, who in *The Diary of a Country Priest* has portrayed a defrocked priest who finds a genuinely human existence outside the church. There he can help people as another person, without the encumbrances of irrelevant creeds or priestly functions. The country priest dies, saying: "All is grace." Some people today do not want to remain within the structures of the church to help others. In the Peace Corps, the Job Corps, in medical or welfare work, or in teaching, they are finding a sense of worth as self-giving human beings.

The fourth trend is that which views contemporary life as being beyond the Christian era. Christian norms no longer dominate society. Men are no longer oriented to the Christian past. Albert Camus made this point in *The Stranger*. Meursault, a young man, cannot grieve for his dead mother; he finds only momentary pleasure in an illicit love affair; he is accused of a murder and sentenced to die. A priest comes to see him in his cell, but they are unable to communicate with one another. John Killinger has pointed out in *The Failure of Theology in Modern Literature:* "Significantly, the only time Meursault becomes angry, truly angry, in the whole business of his extermination by the community, is when the priest urges him to confess and be forgiven." * One might say that the condemned man is angry because the priest wants to compel him to accept a world view which he no longer feels is relevant and because the priest will not accept him as he is. This underscores the need for people to communicate with each other honestly, without the burdens of enforced and unnecessary creedal formulations. There are those who maintain that the forms of religion must be adapted to contemporary men if it is to have relevance. Redemption must be concerned with human integrity, identity, and love.

UNCERTAINTY

We live in such a world of uncertainty that no one seems to know what justice is or how to achieve it. Man is keenly aware that knowledge is changing. What is new today may be obsolete next week. Rules and dogmas that were once sacred seem inapplicable to modern situations. One of the facts of our age is change. (*S/R*, 83.) One of the consequences is a pervasive feeling of confusion and insecurity.

This is as true for science as it is for religion. Physicists have found that solid pieces of metal are in reality masses of moving protons and electrons, that spaces exist between them so that the "solids" are only relatively solid. Even in science we live on relativities. A solid is only relatively so in comparison with something else.

The Christian recognizes relativity. He knows that man's knowledge has limits. He knows that man himself will die. But this is the life to which he had been called, and he lives in the midst of its uncertainties. He has faith not in things of this world or of the next but in God who created him to live in this world. He trusts in God who sustains him, whose revelation in Christ releases him from grubby self-centeredness. In the conquest of death, God not only redeems his creation but shows man an ultimate certainty—God himself. In that trust and faith the Christian man lives and dies.

■ Let four persons read aloud, while the remainder of the group follows the text silently, the description of the four trends, pages 181-83. Pause after reading about each trend long enough for class members to record on the following scale their reaction. This trend expresses my view:

1. ___ Not at all ___ Somewhat ___ To a great extent ___ Most nearly
2. ___ Not at all ___ Somewhat ___ To a great extent ___ Most nearly
3. ___ Not at all ___ Somewhat ___ To a great extent ___ Most nearly
4. ___ Not at all ___ Somewhat ___ To a great extent ___ Most nearly

Now form four groups. Each person will be a part of the group representing the view for which he/she marked the scale *most nearly.* Discuss in the groups: Why do you believe you are at this stage in your view of Christianity? What indications do you get through what you read, from other persons, by your reason, or through other influences, that tell you this is where you are?

If you wish, choose a person to make notes about the responses to the questions to share with the entire group.

■ The *forms* that we use to express the faith (like a particular version of the Bible or a certain creed) often get in the way of the central message. Have a symposium. (Several persons present prepared remarks. They need not interact with one another.) These persons should consider the idea that persons resist change in the *forms* for expressing the faith because they fear a tampering with the essence of Christianity. Let each member of the symposium speak about why persons resist change in one of the following: creeds; forms of liturgy and worship; organization of the church;

church architecture; versions of the Bible; phraseology of the doctrines.

As each person speaks let one half of the class listen for clues about the first of the following questions. The other half should listen for clues about the second of the following questions. In each instance, what is the person trying to protect that is essential to the faith? How can one retain the essentials of the faith and yet become able to accept changed forms?

TO BE CALLED BY GOD

How does the man of faith live? He does not look to heaven as an end in itself. Assured of "heaven" through the love and mercy of Christ, he can give himself to the reconciling work of God in the world. This means that in his private and public life he will try to be open to the leading of the Spirit. He will seek to express love and justice in all that he does. (S/R, 84.)

In our age this surely means that Christianity is no longer a private affair. If we are truly convinced that God has shown his love in the life, death, and resurrection of Christ, we can indeed show our gratitude in our private lives. We must.

But to stop there is to destroy the force of the gospel. We must also love our neighbors as we do ourselves. To do this in a society that is increasingly impersonal, men must promote and support political, social, economic, and civil justice. Justice and the rights that accompany it are the reverse side of the coin we call love. Only by promoting both justice and love can one hope to begin to fulfill Christian obligations. One cannot love everybody, for love is particular, but justice applies to all and is the concrete extension of love.

This sign points to the future in which the Christian man works in the created world in which God has placed him. He does not retreat from it. He accepts it with all its uncertainty, confusion, and sinfulness and seeks to infuse it through his own witness with the reconciling love of God.

This work in the world is his calling. He expresses it in the tasks that he performs as a teacher, manager, partner in marriage, baseball player, judge, or as a member of a civic committee. He expresses it with the talents that God has bestowed on him. He does not fold his hands in despair, saying all is nothingness and meaninglessness. He does not abandon life in the world any more than God has abandoned his creation. He does the best he can with the knowledge and the love that he has in the situations that face him.

Risk is involved. One may not be doing what is right. What he does today may tomorrow prove to be wrong. Christianity, however, is not a matter of knowledge, but of love. The Christian must get as much knowledge as he can in order to express love and justice as effectively as possible, but love is primary to knowledge. Love is faith in action. Love is a present affirmation of hope. Faith, hope, and love are bound together, but the greatest of these is love.

Martin Luther rescued Christianity from the mistaken notion of the Middle Ages that one must retreat to a cloister as a nun or a monk, or be a priest engaged in "spiritual" affairs, before he can be fully Christian. This implied that the unordained layman engaged in the work of the world was hardly religious at all. This notion has carried over into modern times in the idea that only a minister is in "full-time" Christian service. This says in effect that Christianity has no relevant place in the world, that in the world one cannot bear witness to reconciling love. It is a monstrous judgment on God who created the world and on Christ who became incarnate because he *loved* the world.

In man's daily work, he affects others more significantly and constantly than in any other capacity. One pressing task for the church is to show the relevance of religion in every profession. This may mean that bankers will need to get together as a group to discuss their particular problems and tensions in relation to the priesthood of all believers, or that real estate brokers will need to do the same. What do these jobs mean in relation to justification by faith? Can ways be found to serve society more effectively? Is profit an end in itself? Are nonwhites treated with dignity and respect?

■ The importance of ministering through one's everyday work is emphasized in the Scriptures. Listen as someone reads aloud Romans 12 and another reads First Corinthians 12.

Now, use "Forms of Mission" (Resource Packet, item 6, record 2). Study the pictures in the book of selected readings entitled *We Have This Heritage* as the record is played. How do the pictures illustrate the Scripture just read? What possibilities for mission come to your mind? The Leaders' Guide in the packet includes specific directions for using the record and pictures.

AN EXTENDED VOCATION

But even the vocational response is not enough in this power-structured world in which we live. Christians must bring their insights to bear on the power structures of our time by the wise use of their money, the vote, the protest, and pressure in its myriad forms. Entrenched force does not readily sacrifice its prerogatives. Christians must be as wise as serpents and as harmless as doves. Pietism will still have its legitimate place among Christians, but to stop there is to render Christianity half relevant. Christians must be for others in the larger contexts of society.

One of the trends of the future, not yet born but struggling to come into being, is the Christian in his extended vocation. In this vocation he will try in concert with secularists to organize pressure groups that will promote justice in a highly impersonalized and mechanistic society. Many people are so occupied with getting more and more profit, often through means that border on illegality, that we become insensitive to the dehumanizing effects of the system in which we operate. Little people get hurt. They lose heart because they see no recourse or refuge.

This is the new face of principalities, powers, and dominions in our time. In John Steinbeck's *Grapes of Wrath* when the farmer wanted to shoot the fellow who had come to plow up his land, he found there was no one to shoot. The man on the tractor was doing his job for a few dollars. The bankers ordered what the stockholders demanded. The stockholders were ordinary citizens in towns throughout the country. The farmer had no one to shoot. This is our modern dilemma. The forces causing the difficulties seem to be invisible.

They are not invisible, however; they are woven into the fabric of our complex, industrialized society. They produce beautiful patterns, but they also leave ragged edges that chafe the sinews of justice. The social problems of today call for men who can analyze our troubles and push through community and governmental reforms and remedies. Racial discrimination, automation, economic determinism, and power politics call for expert attention. In our extended vocations —that is, as members of pressure groups working for justice—we will have to deal with our impersonal society in those areas where power decisions are made. Otherwise, the Christian witness in our world will be sadly lacking in effectiveness. Christians will not be able to do this alone. They will have to team up with secularists and show that justice benefits all.

The times are gone, if indeed they ever were with us in a realistic sense, when men can cope with social ills on an individualistic basis. Thanksgiving and Christmas baskets relieve hunger only temporarily. They do not get at the root of poverty in our society. Christianity that operates on the "Dial-a-Prayer" level is woefully inadequate. Christians will have to find ways to make Christ relevant to what goes on in General Motors, IBM, and Standard Oil. Such industries shape our lives in multitudes of seemingly unrelated ways. Despite the apparent success in our time of such magnetic figures as Billy Graham and Oral Roberts, revivalism and pietism do not meet the needs of twentieth-century man. (S/R, 85.)

Out of sheer necessity, Christians will have to be in the

world with secularists working for justice. In this they will have to be as wise as serpents for they will be wielders of power. Important as individualistic reforms in temperance, gambling, smoking, and swearing may be, they leave untouched some basic issues of the future such as relations between races and economic classes and labor-management.

To be in the world for others, to love one's neighbor whom he may never contact, the Christian will have to deal with centers of power decisions. This means striving for political freedom and social equity through our lawmaking bodies, our courts, job agencies, ghetto programs, educational policies, antipoverty drives, funds for investment, demonstrations, and strikes. This also means mastering the techniques of applying power in local, national, and international situations. (S/R, 86.) Gandhi knew this technique when he marshaled world opinion and sympathy for the downtrodden Indians.

The faithful use of power may require shifting from the individual to larger and larger power groups to which the world will listen. This is evident in the news coverage given to papal pronouncements but not to pronouncements of the Methodist Council of Bishops or the Southern Baptist Convention. The pope's decisions affect millions more. Lifting the ban on meat on Friday affects large economic blocks of society. These are the ingredients to which the world pays attention. Moralizing finds little acceptance. In many cases, legal procedure is required before injustices can be corrected. Sermons can easily be dismissed, but a court order cannot.

To engage in such uses of power is not to abandon the love ethic of Christianity. It is to apply it realistically. Christians will need to have groups organized to watch for points of encroachment on individual and social rights, like the Institute for American Democracy which keeps tabs on extreme left and right wing groups to counteract their propaganda and expose their true purposes.

189

■ Why is it that persons interested in working for justice or bringing about change in society have sought to act through organizations other than the church? Pierre Berton says, "In those basic conflicts that ought to be tormenting every Christian conscience . . . the Church has trailed far behind the atheists, the agnostics, the free thinkers, the journalists, the scientists, the social workers, and even, on occasion, the politicians." (See S/R, 80.) Let members of the class cite aloud the reasons why they think persons work through organizations other than the church. Have someone record the reasons on chalkboard or newsprint as they are listed. How did the church contribute to the apathy and disillusionment talked about in the last paragraph of S/R, 80? In what ways is the church today contributing to disillusionment and apathy? Compare the views in this selected reading and those presented in this book with those in S/R, 82. Which most nearly expresses your feelings? Why?

■ Signs pointing to the future call for concentrated effort in and through the church. (See pages 187-89 of this chapter and S/R, 86.) Form groups of four to six persons. Each group should choose one of the following descriptions of the church to discuss.

What would the church be like if we thought of it as: (1) An army of Christian soldiers? (2) A well-run business? (3) A school? (4) An Olympic track team? (5) A small urban community? (6) A family?

Consider each description in the light of some of these questions: What would be the goals? the methods of operation? the types of relationships between people? the styles of leadership? the kinds of resources needed? the possible forms of organization? Through your consideration of the questions, what clues do you find for making the church, as it is presently operating, more influential in society? Let this question form the basis for a report from your group to the entire class.

The church of the future will surely serve as a "hot line" center to note danger points. It will probably be a large center from which many activities will emanate. The small church as essentially a preaching station will disappear. The ministry of the rural church will be expanded to help persons meet their total needs; persons in the town and country areas need a seven-days-a-week ministry, not just an hour or two on Sundays. Rural group ministries will grow. These small church and rural ministries will be related to the multiple ministries and the special missions sent forth from the large centers. Specialized group ministries will increase in